GREENHOUSE GARDENING
GARDENING
& GROWING UNDER GLASS

KENNETH A. BECKETT

TREASURE PRESS

Early vegetables – see pages 56-7

Contents

Illustrations by

Jillian Burgess: David Salariya 6-9, 34-47
The Garden Studio: Christine Davison 70-81
   Liz Pepperal 58-69
   Nina Roberts 82 91
Hayward Art Group 10-21
Sandra Pond 4-5, 22-33, 94-5
Carole Vincer 2, 50-7

First published in Great Britain in 1982 by
Octopus Books Limited

This edition published in 1987 by
Treasure Press
59 Grosvenor Street
London W1

© 1982 Hennerwood Publications Limited

ISBN 1 85051 177 2

Printed in Hong Kong

THE BUILDING

THE STRUCTURE Amateur gardeners grow plants under glass for a variety of reasons. The commonest is the wish to have fresh, home-grown tomatoes, cucumbers, lettuces, grapes, or peaches. Many people also enjoy growing flowering pot plants or cut flowers, or like to have a place where they can keep house plants that are resting or need resuscitating. Whatever the motivation, however, greenhouse gardening should not be embarked upon without a good deal of planning. After all, it depends upon creating and maintaining an environment that is quite different from the one outside the glass walls, and juggling with artificial or natural heat sources and ventilating and shading systems is not always easy. Luckily, many of the most popular greenhouse plants have a wide tolerance – and most of the environmental controls can be automated if the added cost is thought to be worthwhile.

THE IDEAL GREENHOUSE

The drawing on these two pages is of an ideal greenhouse: it features not only all the essential equipment but also many of the most valuable but non-essential items. The total cost of such a greenhouse of perfection would be very great – and a quite unnecessary luxury for the beginner.

For the ideal greenhouse a traditional oblong box-shaped house with a span roof has been chosen. The structure is of red cedar, a rot-proof timber of pleasing colour that needs only a coat of linseed oil every five years to keep it in good condition.

How big the greenhouse should be is largely dictated by how much space you have available in the garden and how much money you are prepared to spend. These considerations aside, however, it is always best to go for one which is bigger than seems necessary; the larger it is, the cheaper will be each unit of growing space. An alternative is to choose a model that you can easily enlarge by bolting on extra sections when you need more space. As a rough guide, a 1.8 x 2.4 m (6 x 8 ft) greenhouse is needed to provide enough tomatoes and cucumbers for a family of four.

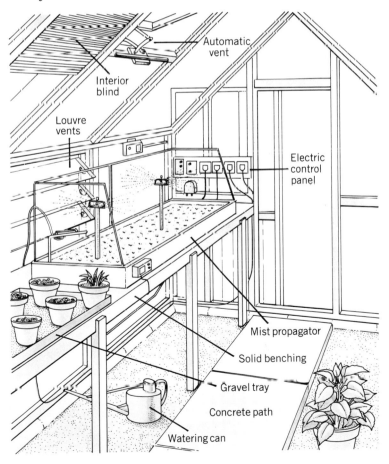

GREENHOUSE DESIGNS
Although there are many other designs, those illustrated here give an idea of the range available. Apart from shape, selection is a matter of choosing between a timber and an aluminium alloy frame. Alloy frames are very durable, require little or no maintenance, and the slender glazing bars allow maximum light admission. Metal is, however, a better conductor of heat and cold than wood. Consequently, more heat is lost from the structure of an alloy house than from a wooden one. The heat loss can be considerable if the greenhouse has to be kept warm in winter, but at other times of the year the loss is unimportant. Another point in favour of wood is the ease with which wire supports, hanging baskets, and extra shelving can be secured to it. Alloy frames are often drilled to allow such accessories to be installed, but the holes are not always exactly where one would like them – and you would need a power drill to make extra ones.

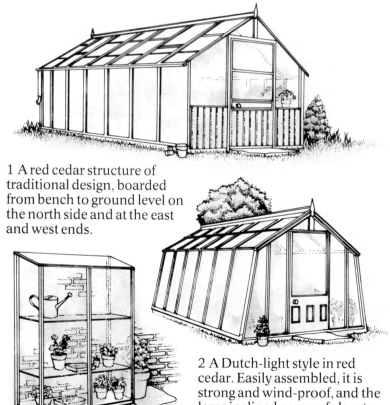

1 A red cedar structure of traditional design, boarded from bench to ground level on the north side and at the east and west ends.

2 A Dutch-light style in red cedar. Easily assembled, it is strong and wind-proof, and the large inclined panes of glass to ground level allow maximum winter sunlight to enter.

3 A very small wood-framed lean-to design. This is ideal for restricted areas, taking up little room and reaping the benefit of extra heat from the sun-warmed bricks of the house wall.

4 A traditional design in aluminium alloy. The slender beams and glazing bars allow plenty of light to enter.

5 The alloy-framed Hartley design. Its faceted construction allows maximum sunlight to enter.

6 One of the newer circular designs in alloy. It is not only pleasing to look at but very convenient to work in with a minimum of movement.

7 A structure of tubular alloy and polythene sheet.

8 A tunnel house of plastic sheeting and tubular alloy. Both this one and 7 are cheap and easy to erect, but they are liable to wind damage; even if used on sheltered sites, the sheeting will need to be replaced every few years.

CHOOSING THE SITE

The performance of a greenhouse depends greatly on its siting in the garden. It needs to receive long periods of direct sunlight and to be shielded from strong, cold winds. These factors are especially important if winter crops such as lettuce are to be grown. On the shortest day in Britain – 21 December – the sun rises to only about 17 degrees above the horizon at mid-day and casts long shadows. If the greenhouse is acquired in summer, it is possible to discover where the winter shadows will fall by using the simple equipment shown in the drawings. Two pieces of parallel-sided board secured with a nail or screw make an adequate substitute for callipers. The lower arm is kept exactly horizontal and pointed due south. The upper arm is opened out to an angle of 17 degrees to find the height of the winter sun. If solid objects (buildings, conifers) rise above the upper arm's sight-line, the position will be in winter shadow. The longer axis of the house should be aligned east-west. This will reduce to a minimum the shadows cast by the roof supports and glazing bars.

Although winter light is all-important for crops grown during the shortest days, shelter from strong, cold winds is also vital. Heat losses of up to 50 per cent can occur during a cold winter gale. If there is no natural shelter, open-weave fences or hedges should be provided – see drawing, right (though the latter will take several years to become fully established). If winds are especially strong, a windbreak of trees is advisable.

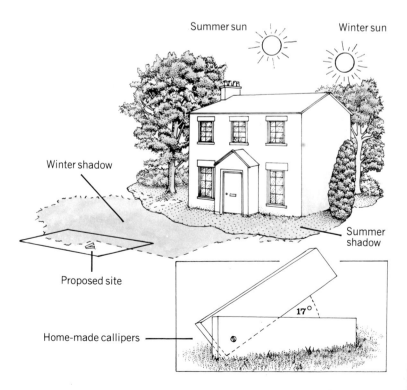

Summer sun

Winter sun

Winter shadow

Summer shadow

Proposed site

Home-made callipers

17°

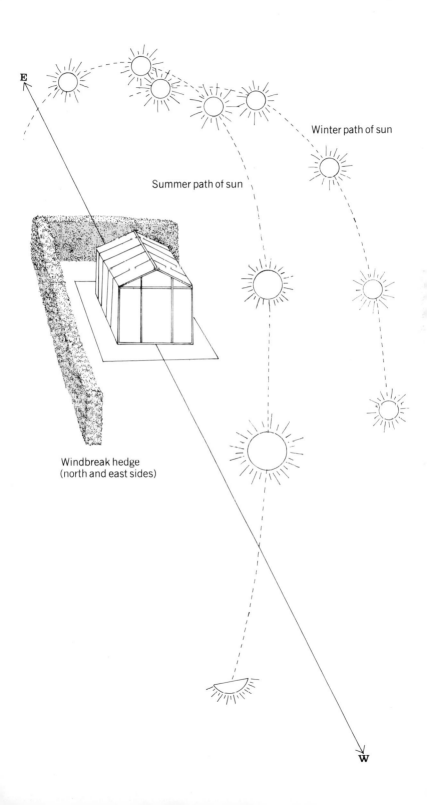

Winter path of sun

Summer path of sun

E

W

Windbreak hedge
(north and east sides)

CONSERVING HEAT
The temperature in a greenhouse or cold frame rises rapidly on a sunny day. The sun's short-wave radiation passes easily through glass and warms all objects it touches. These objects re-radiate warmth in the form of long-wave radiation, which cannot pass through the glass. However, once the sun sets or passes into shadow, heat is soon lost by conduction from glass and framework and by long-wave radiation through the walls and framework; artificial heat is lost in the same way. Heating costs can be reduced by using one of several heat-conservation techniques.

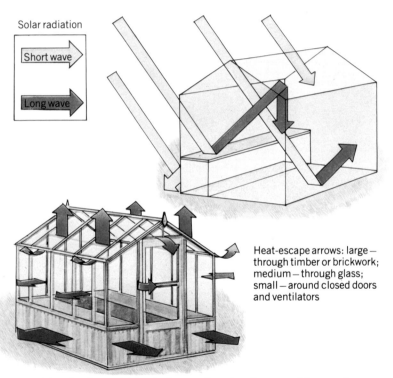

Solar radiation

Short wave

Long wave

Heat-escape arrows: large — through timber or brickwork; medium — through glass; small — around closed doors and ventilators

Double-glazing with polythene sheeting is one of these, the plastic being so secured that there is a gap between glass and sheeting. This does, however, reduce light intensity and encourages condensation, so it is best confined to the coldest sides only. There are various proprietary plastic-glazing products that are attached to the outside of the greenhouse; they prevent condensation and are claimed to make substantial heat savings.

In windy sites there is much to be said for choosing a greenhouse whose walls are bricked or timber-boarded from ground to bench level. Both brick and timber are more efficient than glass as buffers against the wind, and brick in addition can absorb a lot of heat which is re-radiated. Wooden shutters that can be easily but firmly secured in place during the coldest weather are also worth considering.

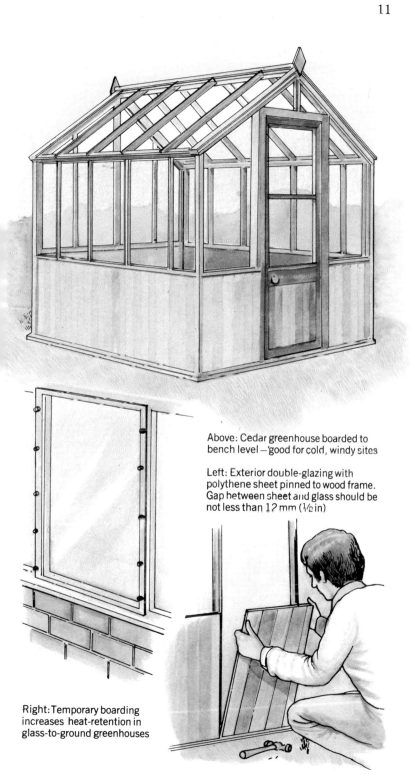

Above: Cedar greenhouse boarded to bench level – 'good for cold, windy sites

Left: Exterior double-glazing with polythene sheet pinned to wood frame. Gap between sheet and glass should be not less than 12 mm (½ in)

Right: Temporary boarding increases heat-retention in glass-to-ground greenhouses

SITE LEVELLING

All custom-built greenhouses are designed to be erected on flat, horizontal ground. If the site is not level it must be made so. Bumpy ground can be levelled by digging out the bumps to fill the hollows, making sure that the completed area is uniformly firmed.

Sloping land can be dealt with by the method shown in the drawing. The site is marked out and a midway line is drawn across it at right angles to the slope. Soil up-slope from this line is excavated and is then deposited down-slope of the line to create a level platform. A straight-edged board and spirit level will be needed to ensure a horizontal finish.

The soil must be thoroughly firmed as work proceeds, preferably with a rammer. Alternatively, the soil should be spread in layers about 100 mm (4 in) deep, each one firmly trodden before the next is applied. If plants are to be grown in the floor of the greenhouse, then it is best to remove the fertile topsoil before levelling the site, and replacing the topsoil when the operation is completed.

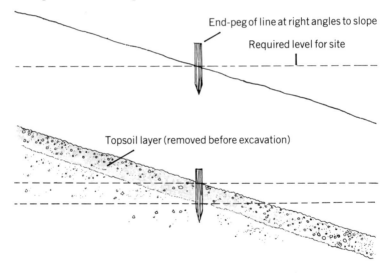

End-peg of line at right angles to slope

Required level for site

Topsoil layer (removed before excavation)

Restored topsoil

Soil from upper slope

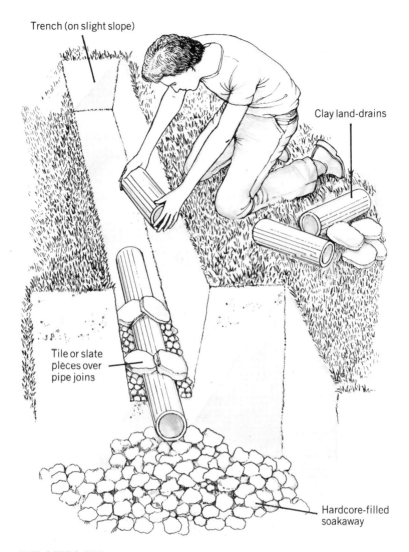

Trench (on slight slope)

Clay land-drains

Tile or slate pieces over pipe joins

Hardcore-filled soakaway

DRAINAGE   A position that is waterlogged or habitually very wet will need to be furnished with some sort of drainage system before it is safe to erect a greenhouse. A row of tile drains below the centre line of the site is easily installed. The drain must have a gentle fall and open into a soakaway or ditch. An alternative is to construct a concrete platform on which to place the greenhouse. Dig out an area about 150 mm (6 in) longer and wider than the greenhouse base and 300 mm (12 in) deep. Fill this with 150-200 mm (6-8 in) of hardcore (broken brick ends or stones) well rammed down and topped off with a layer of concrete. Place wooden shuttering around the sides of the hole so that the concrete platform has a neat edge, and make certain that the surface is level. If the site is really wet the platform should be just above the level of the surrounding soil.

RAINWATER SUPPLY
An ever-present need of the greenhouse gardener is a reliable supply of water, and clean rainwater cannot be bettered. Most custom-built greenhouses offer guttering as an optional extra and it is well worth having. Rainfall can then be easily channelled into tanks or butts ready for use. Butts must have well-fitting lids to keep out dead leaves and other debris that might aid the development of water-borne plant diseases such as damping off. To be worthwhile, two butts each of at least 275 litres (60 gal) capacity will be needed to supply a 1.8 x 2.4 m (6 x 8 ft) house. Butts can take up valuable space outside, so an under-bench or underground location is the ideal solution. Linking pipes to the guttering can easily be taken through the wall or glass.

Unless the storage tanks are large, however, the available rainfall will seldom be sufficient for your needs at the height of the growing season, so it is well worthwhile installing a supplementary mains supply.

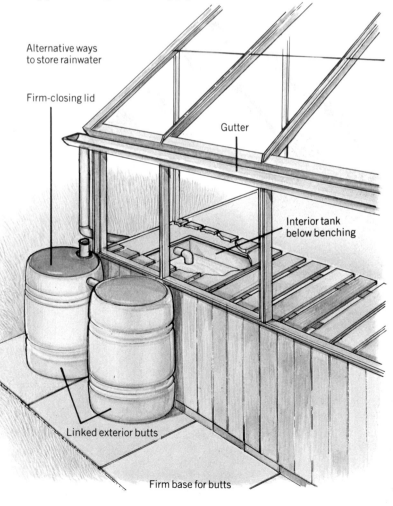

Alternative ways to store rainwater

Firm-closing lid

Gutter

Interior tank below benching

Linked exterior butts

Firm base for butts

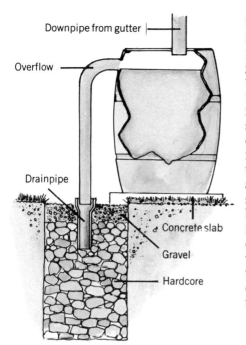

Downpipe from gutter

Overflow

Drainpipe

Concrete slab

Gravel

Hardcore

OVERFLOW Even if mains water is preferred to rain water, guttering is necessary to prevent water pouring off the entire roof length and soaking adjacent paths or flower beds. Piping from the gutters can then carry the water to a properly constructed soakaway or ditch. If butts or tanks are installed, they can overflow during wet weather and should therefore be fitted with overflow pipes leading to a soakaway.

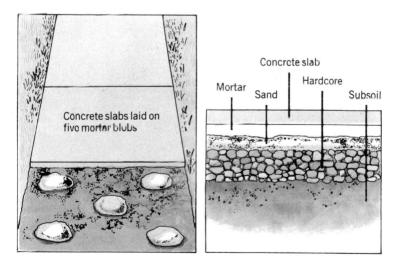

Concrete slabs laid on five mortar blobs

Concrete slab

Mortar   Sand   Hardcore   Subsoil

GREENHOUSE PAVING Whether plants are to be grown in floor-level beds or on benches, there is much to be said for installing a firm, central path in the greenhouse. On well drained soil this can be of paving slabs laid directly on a well-firmed, carefully raked and sanded surface. On the stickier soils a concrete path is recommended. In either case, consider continuing the path across the garden to the dwelling house, thus providing convenient and clean-shod access.

EQUIPMENT

HEATERS Although it is not essential, artificial heat greatly increases the scope of greenhouse gardening. There are five categories of heating: frost-free; cool, night minimum 4-7°C (40-45°F); intermediate 10-13°C (50-55°F), warm 16°C (60°F); and stove 18°C (65°F). The last two are expensive to maintain and, unless truly tropical plants are grown, not essential.

There is a wide choice of greenhouse heaters. Some use solid fuels (coal, coke, wood); others use gas, oil, or electricity. Although the prices of all these fuels are rising rapidly, at the present time solid fuels are a little cheaper than the rest. Whatever the heat source, it must be realised that costs increase steeply with quite modest increments of temperature. It costs twice as much to heat to 13°C (55°F) as it does to heat to 7°C (45°F), and three times as much to heat to 16°C (60°F).

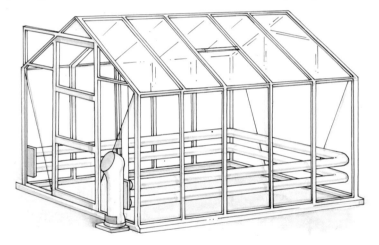

1 A traditional hot-water-pipe system with a modern hopperfed boiler. It is expensive to instal and requires regular maintenance, but it is relatively cheap to run.

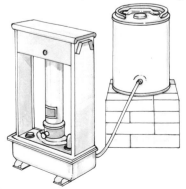

2 A paraffin-oil heater of this design is economical if used just to keep out frost or to maintain cool greenhouse conditions. It must be filled regularly and the wick kept trimmed.

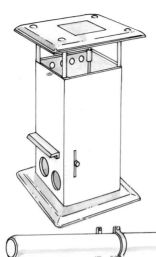

3 Modern thermostatically controlled natural or propane gas heaters are efficient and require little maintenance.

4 Electric (black-heat) tubular heaters. These are an economical way to use electricity, especially if they are thermostatically controlled and used for maintaining frost-free to cool conditions. No maintenance needed.

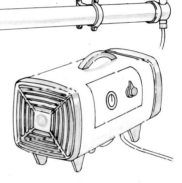

5 An electric fan heater. If coupled to a thermostat, heaters of this kind provide the most convenient and versatile means of warming a greenhouse. Via the fan, heating is almost instantaneous and of a buoyant nature. Maintenance chores are nil bar an annual overhaul.

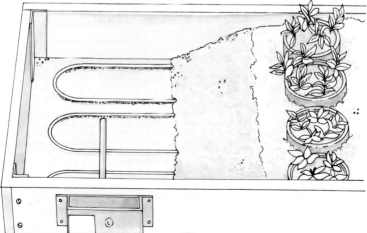

6 Soil-warming cables aid the rooting of cuttings, create optimum soil temperatures for early crops such as tomato, prevent the freezing of soil beds in cold greenhouses, and generally stimulate root activity.

VENTILATORS

Owing to a greenhouse's capacity to retain heat, efficient ventilation is essential. In spite of improvements in the design of small greenhouses in recent years, it is rare to find one with ventilators that are adequate to cope with a really warm summer day. All too often the door has to be used as an emergency ventilator – an inconvenient means, especially in windy weather. Hot air rises, so ridge vents are of prime importance. The total surface area of the ridge vents should be equal to at least one sixth of the floor area. As it rises, the warm air pulls in cooler air from the sides, so vents just above ground and/or at bench level are also essential. Ideally, every other pane along the side of the house should be a vent, although every third one is adequate. All ventilators should open as widely as possible; to get maximum efficiency they need to open through an angle of at least 55 degrees. To conserve heat, ventilators should be under constant control, opening and closing as the sun's heat waxes and wanes. This is seldom possible, especially for people who work away from home, so one of the automatic opening devices is recommended. These can be pre-set to open and close at specific temperatures. Every small greenhouse should have at least two, one on a ridge vent and one at ground or bench level.

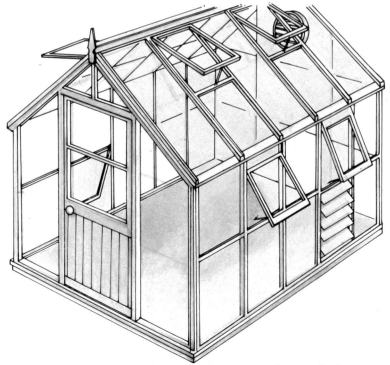

1 Hinged vents on a typical greenhouse. For thorough air circulation the structure needs wide-opening vents, including some at ground level and near the roof ridge.

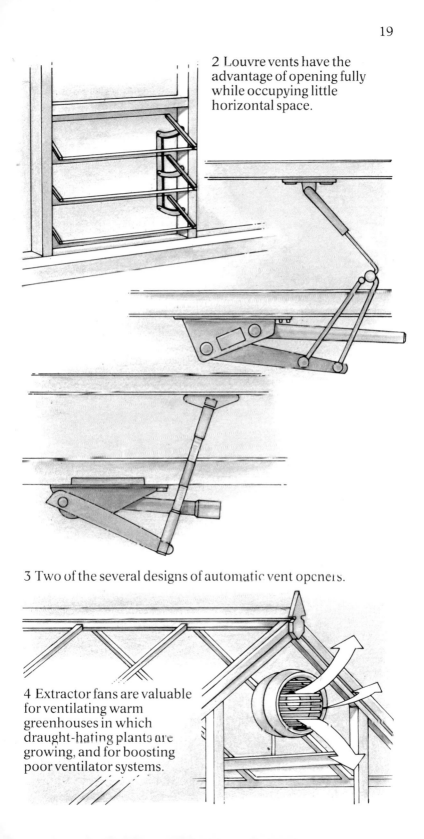

2 Louvre vents have the advantage of opening fully while occupying little horizontal space.

3 Two of the several designs of automatic vent openers.

4 Extractor fans are valuable for ventilating warm greenhouses in which draught-hating plants are growing, and for boosting poor ventilator systems.

SHADES AND BLINDS

During the summer, at least, it is standard practice to shade greenhouses in order to reduce the amount of solar radiation, and thus the intensity of both heat and light, reaching the plants. Shading is useful for a gardener who is away from home all day, especially if the greenhouse has inadequate ventilation. Shading does, however, cut out a lot of the sunlight that is necessary for healthy growth, and so it should be used only when plants need to be protected against direct sunlight. Ferns, orchids, and tropical foliage plants will certainly need shading; most other plants will not, so long as ventilation is adequate.

In the fickle climate of Britain, with its frequent sunless spells in summer, some plants (including tomatoes) may even suffer from lack of light owing to over-shading. There are two basic ways of applying shading: as blinds, or as a coating painted or sprayed directly onto the glass. Although they are more expensive to instal, blinds are greatly to be preferred as they can be easily rolled up or down as required.

1 If you use a proprietary shading compound, choose one of those which can be easily rubbed off when necessary. Lime wash and a well-diluted emulsion paint can also be used, but these are not so easy to remove.

2 Roller types of wooden or plastic slats are the best form of blinds. There are designs for use outside and inside the greenhouse. The latter, although neat and easy to use, can be a nuisance where plants are grown near the glass.

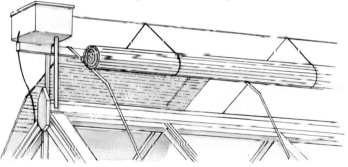

3 The perfect system: mechanised slatted roller blinds automated by linkage with a thermostat, the blinds opening or closing according to the temperature within the greenhouse.

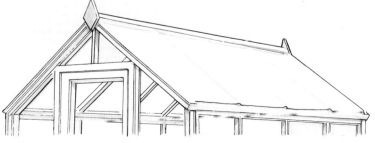

4 Temporary shading provided by old nylon or cotton sheeting. This can be secured directly to the roof or pinned to a framework that can be clipped to the roof.

BENCHING AND SHELVING

Unless you intend to grow plants only in ground-level beds or in large pots or tubs on the floor, you will need to instal benching or staging. This makes watering and general maintenance of pot plants easier, and also brings them nearer to the glass where they benefit from the greater light intensity. Benching should be about waist height and composed of metal or wooden framework and wooden slats. Alternatively, the surface can be of flat or corrugated asbestos or of corrugated galvanised-iron sheeting.

Shelving is mini-benching and is usually secured to brackets at head height or above. It makes use of the roof space and is ideal for seedlings and young plants that need plenty of light, especially in the early months of the year.

Refillable water dispenser

Ballcock valve

Mains header tank

150 mm (6 in) plank parapet

Plastic liner

Sand

CAPILLARY BENCHES
Strong staging is essential if you wish to use a capillary sand bench or trays (these are watering devices which exploit the capillarity of wet sand). Ready-made plastic trays are perfectly adequate for the small greenhouse. Alternatively, the bench sides and ends can be fitted with a parapet at least 60 mm (2½ in) high and lined with heavy-gauge plastic sheeting; this is filled with washed sand, which is kept wet either by can or by a dispenser which works on the same principle as a self-filling bowl for pets. Fully automatic (and fairly expensive) systems involving mains supply, header tank, and ballcock valve deliver water to guttering connected to the edge of the sand bench. Plant pots are pushed into the sand surface with a screwing motion, so that some of the sand is forced into the drainage holes.

WATERING SYSTEM
It takes time and the skill born of experience to keep a collection of pot plants correctly watered: more plants are killed by over- and under-watering than by any other cause. There are now several proprietary automatic watering systems or devices which, although not foolproof, are a boon for the gardener who is away from home during the day. The capillary sand bench or tray method has been dealt with on the previous page. The other types all involve the use of piping attached to a dispenser bottle or to the mains via a header tank and valve. Best known are the trickle systems which, at their simplest, consist of tubes of various bores perforated at intervals. A pot is placed under each perforation and receives a steady drip or trickle of water. Shown here is the more sophisticated system attached to a mains supply.

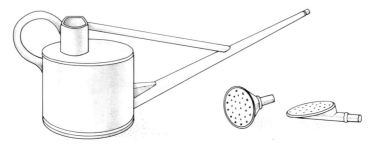

Even if you employ automatic methods of watering, you will still need a watering can for plants on shelving, for applying liquid fertilisers, and so on. A 4.5 litre (1 gal) can like that shown above is the most useful. It should feel comfortable to the grasp, especially when it is raised high to water plants at eye level. A tapered extension spout is useful, and a fine rose for watering newly sown seeds and pricked-off seedlings is essential. Cheap cans seldom last long, so make a point of buying one with a reliable brand name.

THERMOMETER
A maximum/minimum thermometer is indispensable. Suspend it among, or just above, the plants, ideally out of direct sunlight. It should be read daily and the needles re-set. Very high or very low temperatures can cause wilting and scorching. Having a daily record of the maximum and minimum temperature in the greenhouse may enable you to identify their cause.

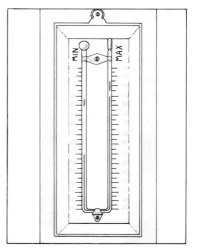

Mains header tank

Water supply to bench

Leads to pots

LIGHTING

In greenhouses which receive poor winter sunlight, artificial illumination provides a valuable boost to seedlings and young plants. The warm white fluorescent tube shown here is easily installed and cheap to run. It is suspended 200-300 mm (8-12 in) above the plant tops and is more efficient if it is fitted with a reflector (you can make a reflector out of aluminium foil). In the larger greenhouse with ample headroom, 400-watt mercury-vapour lamps are ideal, providing both heat and light. They are suspended 1 m (3¼ ft) above the plants.

PROPAGATORS

There is much satisfaction in propagating one's own plants from seeds and cuttings. The seeds of most tender plants need to be germinated at temperatures a little above those needed for the adult plants. Cuttings require a constantly humid atmosphere to enable them to stay alive prior to rooting. For these reasons a well-constructed, heated propagator like the one shown here is well worthwhile. It need not be large or elaborate, and there are models to suit all pockets.

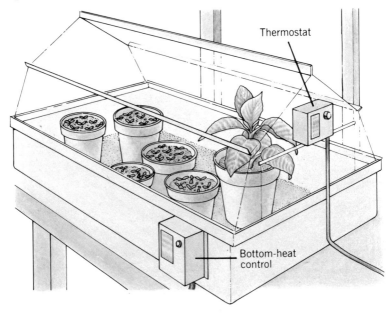

Thermostat

Bottom-heat control

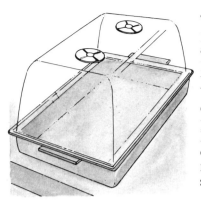

The simple, unheated seed-tray propagator illustrated is cheap, and bottom heat can be provided by a separate heating unit or by soil-warming wires. You can, of course, make your own propagating case using a pot or seed tray, some wire loops, and large polythene bags or sheeting. All propagators must be screened from direct sunshine.

MIST PROPAGATOR
The single-unit mist propagator shown is the last word in propagation equipment. The dedicated gardener will get untold pleasure from it, but its cost is high. Electricity and a mains supply of soft water are required. Cuttings are inserted in sand heated by electric soil-warming cables and kept alive by being bathed in intermittent mist operated by an electronic leaf-and-solenoid valve. Shading is not required and photosynthesis can continue unabated, ensuring rapid rooting.

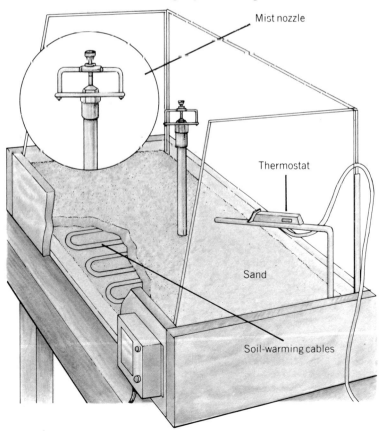

HYGIENE
When glass is dirty, much less light can pass through it, and plant growth is weaker. Even a film of dust can considerably reduce light transmission. Glass should be washed once a year in autumn; but if you live in an industrial area you should wash it at monthly intervals during the winter. As shown here a plant label can be used to clean the grime between the glass overlaps.

Eggs and spores of pests and diseases can lurk undetected on the greenhouse framework, so this should be scrubbed once a year, preferably in early autumn, using a sterilising agent such as Jeyes' Fluid. Ideally, the greenhouse should be empty when this is done.

All pots and boxes should be washed regularly. Do not leave them in untidy heaps with other clutter under the bench, where they could provide a hiding place for pests and diseases.

COMPOSTS To grow good pot plants a properly formulated rooting medium (compost) must be used. Composts must be free-draining and richer than garden soil as the plant roots are closely confined. Approved proprietary composts such as John Innes and the all-peat types are easiest to deal with, but for those who wish to make up their own, the following formula can be recommended. John Innes Potting Compost: 7 parts sterilised loam (ideally top-spit pasture stacked for six months with layers of strawy manure), 3 parts moss peat, 2 parts coarse, washed sand; to each bushel – 560 mm (22 in) x 250 mm (10 in) x 250 mm (10 in) – add 114 g (4 oz) John Innes base fertiliser and 21 g (¾ oz) ground chalk or limestone. Alternatively, an acceptable compost can be produced by adding the John Innes base fertiliser to a mixture of 3 parts moss peat and 1 part sand.

To remove weed seeds and pests, heat the loam to 82°C (180°F), maintain it at this temperature for 10 minutes, then cool it rapidly. This can be done, as shown, in a domestic steamer. Dry, sieved loam is placed in a 150 mm (6 in) layer and about 50 mm (2 in) of water is brought to the boil. A sugar thermometer will be needed, and the temperature should not much exceed 82°C.

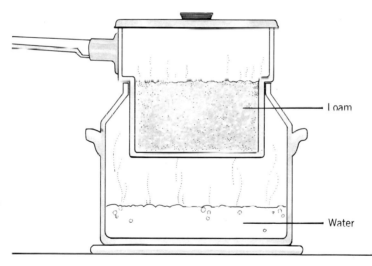

Loam

Water

MIX-YOUR-OWN COMPOST FORMULA

Parts per volume	7 sterilised loam 3 moss peat 2 coarse sand	
plus	114 g (4 oz) J. Innes base 21 g (0.75 oz) chalk	per 0.04 m³ (1 bushel) of compost
or	3 kg (6.5 lb) J. Innes base 0.6 kg (1.3 lb) chalk	per 1 m³ (1.3 cu yd) of compost

CONTAINERS A wide range of containers for growing plants is available, those shown here being the most useful. Indispensable are the traditional flower pots of either clay or plastic. The following sizes will be needed most often and it is worth having a stock to hand: 50 mm (2 in), 60 mm (2½ in), 100 mm (4 in), 125 mm (5 in), 150 mm (6 in); these measurements are of the inside diameter of the rim. If chrysanthemums and other large plants are regularly grown some 200 mm (8 in) and 250 mm (10 in) containers will be required. For seed sowing, half-pots or pans are best, 100 mm (4 in) and 150 mm (6 in) being most useful. For pricking-off more than a dozen seedlings, seed trays about 350 x 200 mm (14 x 8 in) will be essential.

For young plants soon to be placed in the greenhouse border or outside, there are alternatives to traditional pots and boxes. Among the most reasonably priced are the black polythene sleeve pots. Although it is usual to slit these when planting out,

Plastic pot

Clay pot

Half pot

Plastic pans

Square pots

Plastic tray

with care they can be slipped off the root ball and used again. Paper and peat pots are both disposable; they are left in place when planting out, and will eventually rot into valuable humus. Very popular at the present times are the compressed peat-compost pellets, which quickly swell in water to be ready for individual sowing or for pricking-off seedlings or cuttings.

Machines are now available for compressing loam-based and all-peat composts into blocks. These are ideal for use with bedding plants, young tomatoes, cucumbers, and other crops. The various types of hand-made loam-based and all-peat compost blocks require to be handled much more carefully than conventional containers. As the blocks are made they are placed in batches in seed trays, where they remain until the young plants are ready for setting out. Take particular care to water them little but often, with a fine-rosed can. If allowed to dry out, the peat blocks in particular are almost impossible to re-wet properly.

Peat-block compressor

Peat blocks

Polythene sleeve

Peat pot

Peat seed pot

Paper pot

Peat pellets

Peat in plastic net

GROWING BAGS

Among the most popular of the newer aids to gardening are the plastic growing bags – bolster-shaped plastic sacks loose-filled with all-peat compost. They are laid in the growing position and slit beneath at the sides for drainage. Depending on the type of crop grown, panels of various sizes are cut on the upper surface to take the young plants. Being sterile and weed-free they are ideal for crops such as tomatoes (as above, left) and cucumbers.

HANGING BASKETS

Some of the most decorative greenhouse plants have a trailing or pendulous habit and are best displayed in hanging baskets. These can occupy the roof space very pleasingly where headroom permits; alternatively they can be hung outside during the summer or used in the home. While the moss-lined, open-mesh baskets are best for plants such as *Columnea*, there is much to be said for the solid-walled plastic models (see below) now freely available. These have a built-in drip tray and dry out less quickly.

RAISED BEDS If your greenhouse is built on a concrete
platform, or if the soil is wet and sticky, raised beds are an
answer to the problem of growing the larger vegetable, fruit,
and flower crops. These beds should be at least 300 mm (12 in)
deep and edged with a low brick wall, concrete sill, asbestos
sheeting, or (as here) retaining boards. A suitable rooting
mixture can be made of 4 parts garden soil to 1 part of
well-rotted manure, garden compost, or peat and general
fertiliser.

Bench beds are like those for a capillary sand bench (page
23), but with sides at least 150 mm (6 in) deep. They are ideal for
alpines in pans, which can be plunged in deep shingle. Filled
with soil or compost they are equally good for winter lettuce,
cucumbers, and melons.

TECHNIQUES

PROPAGATION Raising plants from seed is a basic operation and is not difficult if you follow the sequence shown in the drawings. For small quantities pots or pans may be used. A John Innes Potting No 1 or seed compost is recommended. Drainage material is not needed in shallow containers. The box or pot is loosely filled proud of the rim; then with a large label or batten the surplus is struck off with a sawing motion. A presser or smaller box or pot bottom is used for light firming, but peat composts should not be firmed. Small seeds are sprinkled thinly, larger ones are best space-sown at about 20 mm (¾ in) apart each way. The seeds are covered with a layer of compost equal in depth to their diameter and strained through a fine sieve. Very fine seed such as begonia is best mixed with 30-50 parts by bulk of dry sand and sown without

Growing from seed: take off surplus compost from tray.

Sprinkle small seeds thinly over surface of compost.

Cover seeds with very thin layer of sieved compost.

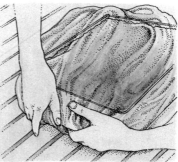

Water seeds, then put tray in transparent plastic bag.

further covering. After sowing, water the seeds either with a fine-rosed can or by partial immersion in a bowl of water. The box or pot is then covered with a pane of glass or a plastic bag and kept out of direct sunlight or shaded with sheets of newspaper. Most seeds will germinate satisfactorily at a temperature of 16-18°C (60-65°F).

LAYERING

This is one of the most reliable methods of propagating carnations, shrubs, and climbers. Low stems are pulled to ground level and bent into a U-shape. The bottom of the U is cut half through and covered with compost until rooting occurs.

Air layering is carried out on stiff-stemmed plants, preferably in the spring. The operation is clearly shown in the drawings. The wound should be dusted with hormone rooting powder and wedged open. Polythene sheeting or sleeving is used. A suitable compost is made up of equal parts of moist moss and peat or a potting compost.

Air layering: 1 Make upward cut. 2 Wedge cut open, dust with rooting powder. 3 Fill plastic tube with moss, then tie ends.

4 When roots show through moss, cut shoot off parent.

5 Pot the new plant in a good quality potting compost.

CUTTINGS These are severed pieces of stem, leaf, or root that are induced to produce shoots and roots and to form young plants. **Leafy cuttings** require a humid environment, for which a propagating case or mist unit is necessary (see pages 26-27). Coarse washed sand or equal parts of this and moss peat makes a good rooting medium. Healthy **stem tips** provide the best cuttings of soft stemmed plants such as *Pelargonium* (see page 74). They should be about 60 mm (2½ in) long with the lower leaves removed and the stem cut cleanly with a sharp knife or razor blade immediately below the basal joint. Cuttings of shrubs and climbers, as shown here, should be about 75 mm (3 in) long and have the soft tip removed. Some shrubs and climbers root best if the cutting includes a 'heel' of wood from the parent stem. A hormone rooting powder is recommended. Cuttings are inserted up to the first leaf – about halfway up – and watered in. They should be sprayed with a fungicide such as benomyl to prevent early rotting.

The bare leggy stems of old *Dracaena* and *Dieffenbachia*

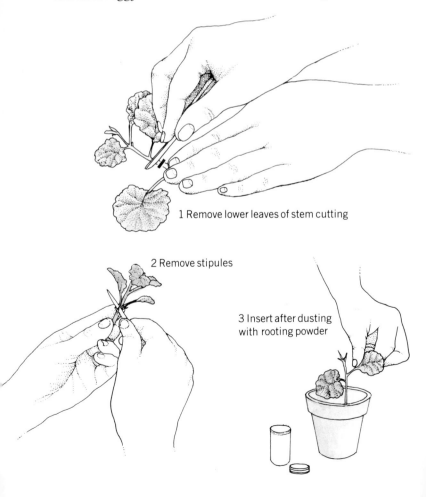

1 Remove lower leaves of stem cutting

2 Remove stipules

3 Insert after dusting with rooting powder

plants can be cut into 50 mm (2 in) lengths to make
stem-section cuttings. These are inserted vertically or
horizontally with sides or tops flush with the sand and kept at
18-24°C (65-75°F). Plants with many stems at ground level can
be divided, by pulling or cutting into rooted portions. Some
plants produce suckers – rooted shoots from below ground
level – which can be uncarthed, severed from the parent and
potted separately.

The India-rubber plant *(Ficus elastica)* and some others
grow from **leaf-bud cuttings,** single leaves with a 25 mm (1 in)
section of stem, treated the same way as ordinary leaf cuttings.
Saintpaulia, Peperomia, Sansevieria, and many succulents are
propagated by single leaves or leaf sections as shown here.

Many hardy plants and some greenhouse ones can be raised
from **root cuttings,** including *Pelargonium* and *Passiflora.*
Roots at least 2.5 mm (1/10 in) thick are chosen and cut into
50-75 mm (2-3 in) lengths, which are laid horizontally, just
covered with compost, and kept at about 16°C (60°F).

Leaf cuttings (*Begonia*): cut
across veins on underside, then
pin leaf topside up to compost

Stem cuttings
(*Dieffenbachia*):
only tops should
be visible

PRICKING-OFF

Seedlings, especially if they were thickly sown, must be separated as soon as possible if they are to grow on without a check. The time to do this is when the seed leaves have expanded but before the true leaves fully develop. Seedlings are best spaced 40-50 mm (1½-2 in) apart in boxes as indicated in the drawing.

A blunt-pointed stick is used, and the operation is known as pricking-off. Take great care when handling the seedlings to avoid damaging the roots. Make as deep a hole as possible, lower a seedling into it, and fill the hole and gently firm it with a sideways motion of the dibber. Seedlings as large as tomatoes, for example, can be pricked off singly into small pots, peat pellets, or soil blocks.

POTTING

When the pricked-off seedlings are growing well and as soon as the leaves just start to overlap, they must be separated again and potted singly. The separation must be done with care so that each young plant has a ball of roots and compost. Pots are chosen which allow at least a 20 mm (¾ in) gap between the root ball and the pot wall. It has been established experimentally that, provided the compost is properly made, no special drainage material is needed when potting. However, one crock over large drainage holes may be necessary to prevent fine compost from leaking out. Each pot is filled to about one third of its depth with compost, and the plant is set on this and then filled around with more compost (see below). The pot should be rapped two or three times on the bench top, then gently firmed with the finger tips (all-peat composts should not be firmed). The young plant should sit at the same level as, or a little deeper than, it was before. A gap must be left for watering between the compost surface and the pot rim (see diagram, below left). As a rough guide this gap should be equal to about one seventh of the pot depth. When watering seedlings you should always use a fine-rosed can.

POTTING-ON In general, when the young plant is growing vigorously and has filled its pot with roots, it needs a larger container if it is to continue to increase its size in the normal way. The procedure is known as potting-on. A larger pot is selected to allow at least a 25 mm (1 in) gap between the root ball and pot side. The plant to be potted-on is inverted onto the open hand with the stem hanging between the middle and index fingers. The pot rim is rapped gently but firmly onto a wood surface and the pot should then lift off easily (below, left). Enough compost is now placed in the new pot to bring the top of the root ball to the right level for watering (see previous page). The gap between the side of the pot and the root ball is filled in with compost and gently firmed with the fingers, so that it is level with or just above the top of the root ball (below, right). Watering should be with a fine-rosed can.

RE-POTTING In certain cases it may be necessary to prevent a perennial plant, shrub, or climber from growing any larger. These plants will need to be periodically re-potted – that is, transferred to another pot of the same size. Re-potting gives you the opportunity to provide the plant with fresh soil and to rejuvenate its root system and – with the help of some pruning – to keep it to the same size as before. During the dormant season the plant is knocked from its pot and the root ball is evenly reduced by about a quarter with the aid of a hand fork, the thick roots being cut away with secateurs (below). A clean pot of the same size is used and the plant dealt with as described under potting-on. If large plants are being re-potted, a potting stick may be useful to push the compost down evenly so that air pockets do not occur. (A potting stick is a batten twice as long as the pot is deep and of finger thickness.)

TOP-DRESSING
Shrubs, climbers, and perennials, especially those growing permanently in large containers, benefit from an annual top-dressing (below). During the dormant season the top layer of soil and fine roots is stripped away (the thicker roots that go straight down must not be severed). This layer should not be more than one sixth the depth of the root ball. It is replaced immediately by a rich compost, such as John Innes Potting No 2 or 3, or by a 50/50 mixture of rotted manure and good garden soil.

The permanent borders in the greenhouse should also be top-dressed annually. It is not usually necessary first to remove any topsoil or roots from ground-level beds, although if the soil level in raised beds is high the top 25 mm (1 in) or so can be stripped with a rake.

FEEDING Top-dressing alone is seldom enough to keep long-term pot plants and those permanently in beds and borders growing healthily. Many short-term plants (those grown as annuals or biennials, such as *Calceolaria*, *Chrysanthemum*, and *Schizanthus*) also soon exhaust the supply of essential mineral foods in the compost. In both cases, to maintain vigour and abundant blooming, you will have to give the plants a supplementary feeding (above).

Suitable fertilisers can be applied in three ways: dry to the soil, liquid to the soil, and liquid to the leaves. All types can be bought ready to use and should be applied strictly according to the makers' instructions. Dry mixtures are best for beds and borders, but the quick-acting liquid feeds are recommended for plants growing in containers. Quickest of all are the foliar feeds, highly solvent compounds that are sprayed onto the leaves. They are very useful for short-term pot plants that are showing signs of starvation.

WATERING

All actively growing plants in containers need regular watering, and this must be done thoroughly, filling up the space between the soil surface and pot rim. This ensures the moistening of the whole root ball. If you have doubts as to whether a plant needs water, there are two easily recognisable symptoms that you can look out for. A slight but unnatural nodding of soft stem and leaf tips is often the first visible effect of water shortage. If the compost is pale and dry-looking on the top, water is usually needed; scratching with the finger tip will show whether or not the soil is moist below the surface. In general, if you are in doubt as to whether to water: in winter, do not; in summer, do.

DAMPING DOWN

Most greenhouse plants benefit from a humid atmosphere when they are actively growing. This is easily provided by damping down – that is, wetting the floors, walls, and benches at least once a day as soon as the temperature rises above 13-16°C (55-60°F).

PLANT SUPPORTS

Tomatoes, melons, cucumbers, and ornamental climbers all need supporting. The best method is to instal permanent horizontal galvanised wires attached to vine eyes or to holes drilled in the framework of alloy greenhouses. A typical support system for a vine is shown in the drawings on the opposite page. Vertical string can be tied to the wires for twining climbers. Alternatively, large-meshed green plastic netting or trellis can be used. Many smaller plants in pots also need supporting. Very slender or split canes or twiggy sticks should be used. They are inserted directly into the containers. It is important to make this kind of staking as unobtrusive as possible, and to secure the plants neatly with fine green twine, raffia, or one of the soft wire ties. This pepper (right) has a central cane and side ones to support the largest fruits.

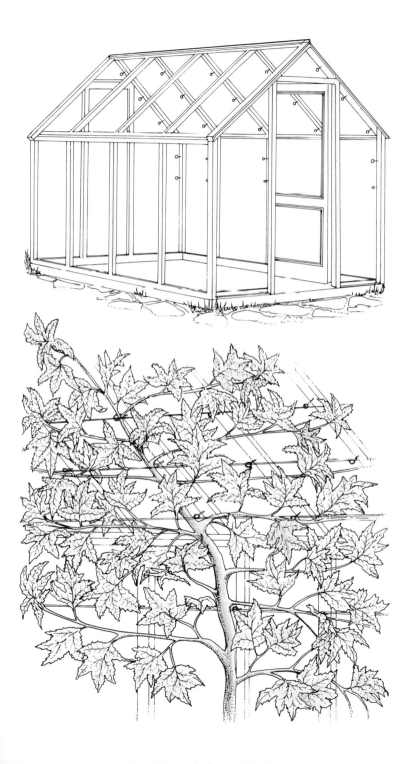

PRUNING

Whether they are large or small, or whether grown in containers or beds, there are few greenhouse plants that do not need some kind of pruning – that is, the removal of shoots or stems for a definite purpose (as below, with *Impatiens*). The primary purposes of pruning are to train a plant into a particular form, as in the case of a cordon grape-vine or a fan-trained peach; to initiate branching and bushiness, as with *Chrysanthemum* and geraniums; or merely to curtail exuberant growth, as with many shrubs and climbers.

The various training types of pruning are described or illustrated with the relevant crops. Whatever is intended, it should be done with care. Sharp secateurs should be used and the cuts made neatly immediately above a leaf or bud. If a long snag or ragged end is left the stem may die back.

PINCHING-OUT

This is the term used when the tips of soft stems are removed with the nails of the thumb and forefinger. It is particularly used on plants such as *Coleus* and (as here) *Impatiens* to stimulate the development of side branches and so encourage a bushy habit.

TRAINING The pruning of shrubs and climbers in order to train them to develop a particular shape can be a complicated business that takes place over several seasons. To create a single-stemmed plant known as a cordon (as with the grape-vine) you begin by cutting the one-year-old stem or rod back to firm brown-skinned wood. When the young shoots are about 50 mm (2 in) long, all are removed except the strongest, topmost one. This is tied to the wires as it grows. In the following autumn it is cut back as before and all side stems are cut to two basal buds. Once this main stem reaches the end of the greenhouse, all further top and side growth is cut back to two buds annually.

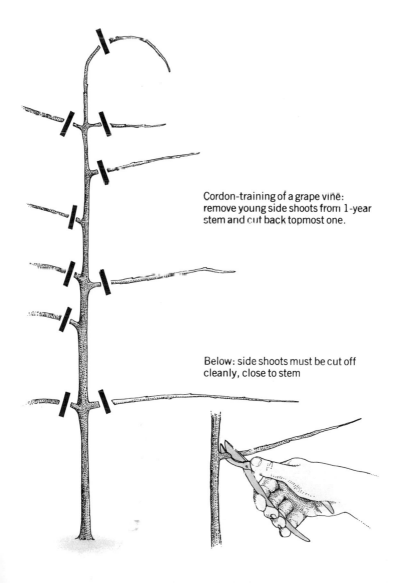

Cordon-training of a grape vine: remove young side shoots from 1-year stem and cut back topmost one.

Below: side shoots must be cut off cleanly, close to stem

PRODUCE

NAME

Begonia, tuberous
Begonia, fibrous (winter)
Begonia, fibrous (summer)
Bulbs, hardy
Bulbs, tender
Calceolaria
Carnation (*Dianthus*)
Chrysanthemum
Cineraria (*Senecio*)
Climbers, ornamental
Cucumber
Cyclamen (seeds)
Cyclamen (corms)
Early vegetables
Fig
Forced asparagus

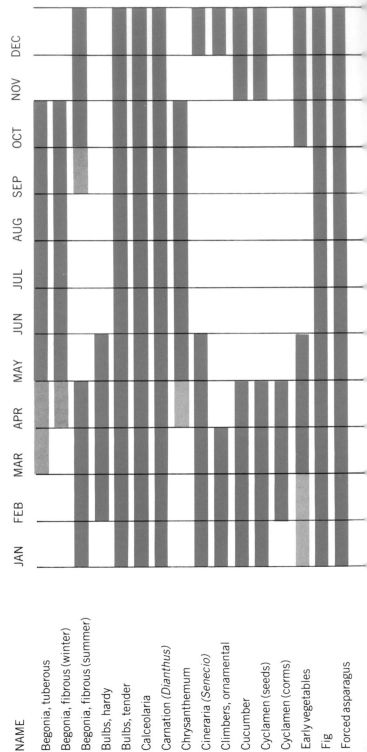

GREENHOUSE CROPPING CHART

JAN FEB MAR APR MAY JUN JUL AUG SEP OCT NOV DEC

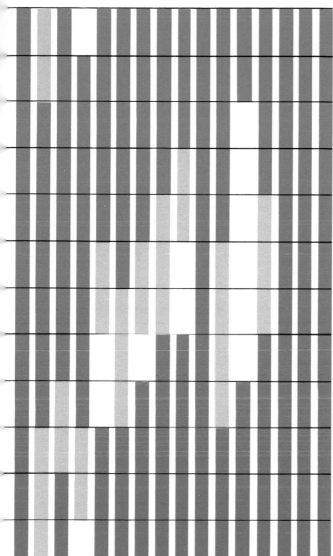

	JAN	FEB	MAR	APR	MAY	JUN	JUL	AUG	SEP	OCT	NOV	DEC
Forced chicory												
Forced rhubarb												
Forced seakale												
Fuchsia												
Grape												
Lettuce												
Melon												
Orchids												
Peach/nectarine												
Pelargonium, geranium												
Primula malacoides												
Primula obconica												
Schizanthus												
Strawberry												
Succulents, cacti												
Tomato												

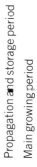

Propagation and storage period

Main growing period

TOMATO Although the tomato is prone to several diseases and is sensitive to cold, it is not difficult to grow some sort of a crop under glass. For the best results, the cultural points outlined here should be followed. The temperature at night must not fall below 7-10°C (45-50°F); it should rise by day to at least 16°C (60°F), with ventilation at 21°C (70°F). If your greenhouse is unheated, therefore, you will have to grow tomatoes only as a summer crop.

Seeds are sown at 18°C (65°F) in spring. Seedlings are placed singly in 75 or 90 mm (3 or 3½ in) pots of John Innes Potting No 2. When the seedlings are well rooted and about 300 mm (12 in) tall, put them into final 250 or 300 mm (10 or 12 in) pots containing John Innes Potting No 2 or 3 (two-gallon plastic buckets with drainage holes are a recommended substitute for these larger pots).

At this time 1.5 cm (5 ft) long canes must be inserted and the plants tied to them. Pinch out all shoots that grow in the leaf axils. When the flowers open, tap each truss daily to aid pollination and fruit formation. Once fruits are seen on the first two trusses, begin feeding the plants, preferably with one of the proprietary liquid fertilisers made specifically for tomatoes. If you feed your plants regularly once a week, you will find that up to eight good trusses of fruits can be obtained. Pinch out the plant top one leaf above the eighth flower truss.

Heavier crops can be obtained by growing the plants in the greenhouse borders or growbags, or by using the technique of ring culture (see next page). The plants can be set out in the borders or growbags (below), at 400 mm (16 in) intervals, when they have reached a height of 300 mm (12 in). Border-soil temperature should be maintained at 13°C (55°F) or higher, otherwise growth will be checked. Subsequent culture is as above, but you can expect a dozen trusses on each plant.

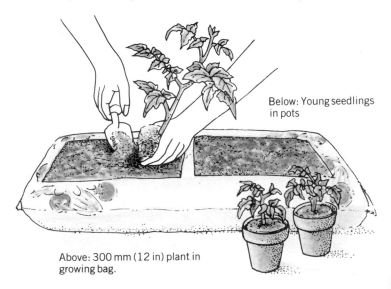

Below: Young seedlings in pots

Above: 300 mm (12 in) plant in growing bag.

Tomato cultivation
Left: pinching growing tip at
eighth flower truss

Below: tapping flower truss to
aid pollination

Right: removing
unwanted
side shoots

Ring culture of tomatoes (above) avoids the problem of root diseases in border soil and gives heavier crops than pot-grown tomatoes. Trenches at least 150 mm (6 in) deep and 400 mm (16 in) wide are dug, lined with plastic sheeting, and filled with a mixture of three parts gravel to one part of vermiculite. Whale-hide rings or bottomless pots 250 mm (10 in) in diameter are placed 150 mm (6 in) apart in the trench, filled with John Innes No 2 or 3, and one plant set in each. Watering at first is into each pot, but when the roots have pushed down into the gravel, all watering and feeding is into this substrate.

You can support the plants by canes or strings; soft hemp string is recommended. This is tied in a loose loop around the stem just below the first true leaf, stretched firmly and secured to a hook or wire above. As the plant grows it is twisted clockwise around the string. Wider-mesh netting can also be used, the tip of the plant being pushed in and out as it grows.

CUCUMBER

The long-fruited greenhouse cucumber needs a minimum temperature of 13-16°C (55-60°F) and a rich rooting medium if it is to do well. Horizontal galvanised wires or wide plastic mesh gives the best support (see page 54). Sow the seeds in spring, singly and edgeways 12 mm (½ in) deep in 60 mm (2½ in) pots of John Innes Potting No 1. Germination requires a minimum temperature of 21°C (70°F), but 26°C (79°F) will speed the process.

When the seeds have germinated, you must make special **growing mounds** (below) for the plants. These may be located in the border soil or on benches; they are disc-shaped, 500-600 mm (20-24 in) wide, and 300 mm (1 ft) apart. First you need to put down a 150 mm (6 in) layer of rotted manure, then a 100 mm (4 in) layer of John Innes Potting No 2, followed by more manure and a topping of compost. Cucumber plants need shading at all times from direct sun, and they appreciate a humid atmosphere. Damping down (see page 44) should be carried out daily once the temperature in the greenhouse rises above 18°C (65°F).

Left: Long-fruited greenhouse cucumber

Growing mound

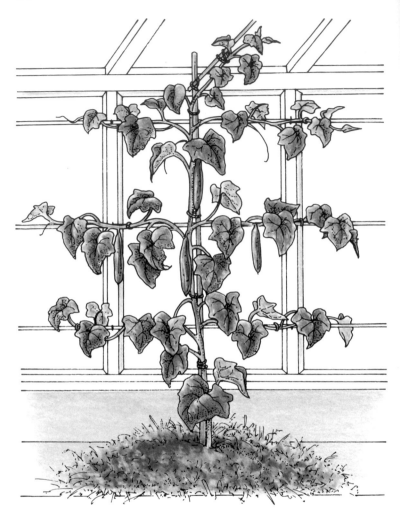

When each cucumber seedling shows the second true leaf, **pot it on** into a 90-100 mm (3½-4 in) pot and support it with a 450-600 mm (18-24 in) high cane. As soon as the plants are about 300 mm (12 in) high, set them one to each mound and tie the canes to the wires or mesh. As the stem grows, secure it vertically to the support and remove all sideshoots from the lower five leaves. Train all the remaining sideshoots horizontally, alternately to left and right, as in the drawing.

When each lateral stem produces a female flower, pinch out its tip two leaves beyond; then, when the shoots from the axils of these leaves in turn produce female flowers, these must be pinched out one leaf beyond, and so on. As soon as the main stem reaches 1.5 m (5 ft), remove its tip, and if there is still head room you can take a lateral stem up to the top of the support when its tip is removed.

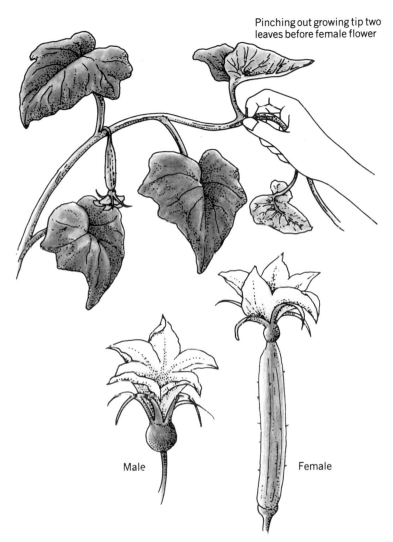

Pinching out growing tip two leaves before female flower

Male

Female

Once young cucumbers start to swell, give them a fortnightly **dressing** of dried blood or fish meal; alternatively, you can give them a liquid feed once a week. As soon as a mesh of white roots shows on the mounds they should be top dressed with compost or manure.

If this mound method of cultivation is not convenient, a smaller but acceptable cucumber crop can be had by growing the plants in 250-300 mm (10-12 in) pots or buckets of John Innes Potting No 2 or 3; growbags have also been used with success.

Cucumbers produce separate male and female flowers, as shown. If you allow pollination to take place you will get thick, bitter fruits, so pick off the male flowers as soon as they show. The cultivar (cultivated variety) 'Femdam' does not produce male flowers.

LETTUCE

Particularly appreciated in winter, lettuces
can be had from November to March if a winter minimum
temperature of 7-10°C (45-50°F) can be maintained and if the
greenhouse receives good winter light. Well-manured beds and
borders are best, but acceptable lettuces can be produced in
deep trays or, singly, in 125-150 mm (5-6 in) pots. For a
succession, sow the seeds in late September, November, and
January at 13-16°C (55-60°F). The seedlings can be pricked-off
into trays at 50 mm (2 in) intervals each way or, ideally, singly
into soil blocks or peat pellets. About a month later they must
be set out, 200-230 mm (8-9 in) apart each way, or placed singly
in final pots. Take care (as in the drawing below) when
watering the plants, especially in winter, not to splash water
onto the leaves as this encourages the formation of grey mould.
Four weeks after setting out, you can begin liquid feeding at 7-
to 10-day intervals. Among the best lettuce cultivars are
'Kordaat' for heated greenhouses and 'Kwiek' for cold ones.

EARLY VEGETABLES

A variety of hardy vegetables can
be had early if sowings are made in late winter or early spring.
Beetroot, carrot, French beans, radish, spinach, and turnip can
all be sown in beds or deep boxes provided there is good light.

OTHER CROPS

Among alternative or additional summer
crops are aubergine (egg plant), bell (sweet) peppers, and
courgettes (marrow). All are sown in spring at 18-24°C
(65-70°F). Courgettes are best sown singly; the others are
space-sown in pans or boxes, then pricked-off singly into peat
pellets or 75 mm (3 in) pots. Courgettes need well-manured soil
– at least one large bucketful per plant – and grow too large for
the small greenhouse. Peppers and egg plants can be grown in
the same way as tomatoes, either as cordons or as bushes. In
the latter case, the tops are pinched out to encourage branching
when the plants are about 150 mm (6 in) high.

Some early greenhouse crops

PEACH AND NECTARINE The peach and its

smooth-skinned form, the nectarine, are rewarding fruit crops
but they do need rather a lot of space: the greenhouse should
not be less than 3.5 m (12 ft) long. The ideal is a lean-to against a
wall 3 m (10 ft) high.

Peaches are grown as fans on walls or on wires beneath
the roof. The soil must be well drained and enriched with
well-rotted manure or with peat plus a general fertiliser applied
at a rate of 90 g/m² (3 oz per sq yd). The best time for planting is
in late October or November, and you will find that
one-year-old trees are cheapest.

After planting, cut back the plant to about 60 mm (2 ft).
Of the shoots that follow, select two that grow in opposite
directions and tie them to the wires at an angle of 45 degrees.
At the end of the year, cut them back to 450 mm (18 in).
Subsequently, retain three shoots on each stem and tie them in
evenly in fan formation.

This pruning pattern continues until the tree has developed
about 32 main branches. These can then be allowed to grow on
to fill the allotted space in the greenhouse. Thereafter, carry out
all the main pruning in summer.

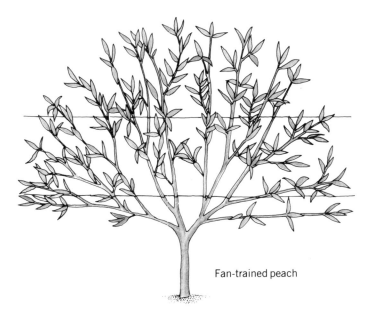

Fan-trained peach

Pollinating peach flowers

Below: peach (left) and nectarine

For an early crop the greenhouse must be heated to a minimum of 5-7°C (41-45°F) from late January. If no heat is available, keep the greenhouse shut, ventilating it only when the temperature rises to 18°C (65°F). When the flowers bloom, pollinate them daily with a small, soft-haired paint brush or with a rabbit's tail; it will help if you dampen the greenhouse floor afterwards, and close the door for a short while in order to raise the temperature.

Flowers and fruits are carried on the previous season's stems, and the object of pruning is the regular production of these stems. As shown right, above, all shoots on the fruiting stems are removed except a strong shoot below the first fruitlet and the topmost shoot. When the fruit is picked, the stem which bore it is cut back (right, below) and the young stem below it is then tied into its place. Watering must be regular and thorough during the growing season. A manure mulch or a dressing of general fertiliser should be applied in May.

GRAPES

Fine-quality grapes can be grown in a cold or cool greenhouse, but like peach trees the grape vine needs plenty of room. There is little point in trying to grow a vine in a structure less than 2.4 m (8 ft) square in floor area.

You will need to instal a system of horizontal wires 300 mm (12 in) apart to support your vine. Buy a one-year-old plant and set it either in the greenhouse border or immediately outside, whence the main stem can be led inside through a hole in the greenhouse wall. The soil must be enriched, ideally with a large bucketful of manure and 114 g (4 oz) of general fertiliser to each square metre. Planting is best done in autumn. For methods of training, see page 47.

Grape-vines when dormant must be kept cold, with the greenhouse vents open during this period. Artificial heat is not needed for the first year or two while the vine is being trained, nor thereafter unless you wish to grow early fruits. Prune the fruiting-sized stems or rods in autumn, and cut back all the side (lateral) stems to two buds.

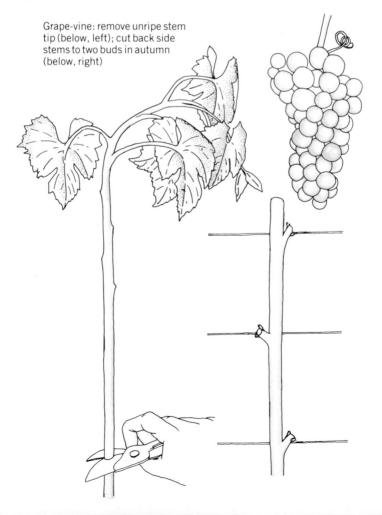

Grape-vine: remove unripe stem tip (below, left); cut back side stems to two buds in autumn (below, right)

Untie the rod and lower it to a horizontal position, with the tip touching the floor: this will encourage the even swelling of buds the following spring. All loose bark should be rubbed off and the rod painted with an insecticide such as malathion. The greenhouse should be closed in late January and ventilated only when the temperature rises above 21°C (70°F). If an early crop is required, you will need to provide a minimum night temperature of 10°C (50°F).

Syringe each of the rods with clean water daily. When the buds break, re-tie the rods and make a point of damping down the greenhouse every day. When the shoots are about 50 mm (2 in) long, select a strong one for each wire alternately to the right and left, and remove the rest.

When the flower trusses show, pinch the stem back to two leaves beyond the second truss. More shoots (sublaterals) will arise from the leaf axils, and these should be pinched back to one leaf. Do not check further growth, but if necessary thin out the plant when the fruits are ripening.

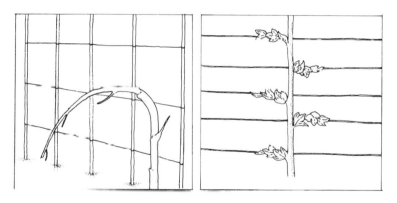

Above, left: tie pruned rods flat. Above, right: tie new shoots in spring.
Below: pinch out tip two leaves beyond flower truss

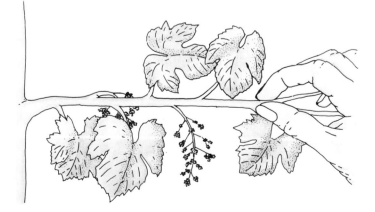

Grape-vines must be watered well throughout the growing season. When the flowers open, however, discontinue damping down, and dust the trusses daily with a camel-hair brush to aid pollination. Then, after the tiny fruits have formed, resume the damping down, and feed the vine every two weeks with a wet or dry fertiliser. When the fruits are as large as peas, thin the more congested clusters with a forked twig and a pair of slender-pointed scissors. Avoid touching the fruits, as this spoils their waxy 'bloom'.

Propagating grape-vines

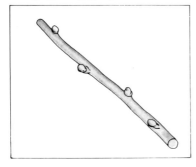

Stem prunings taken in the autumn are partly buried in a shady spot.

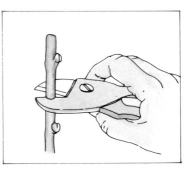

In February cut the prunings into 50 mm (2 in) lengths, each with one 'eye' (bud).

Plant cuttings singly into pots; insert them horizontally, with only the eyes showing.

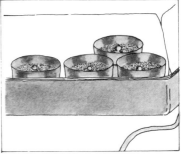

Keep the pots in a propagator at 16-18°C (60-65°F) to encourage rapid shooting.

Fig bush in pot (left) should have shoots pinched back (above) to three leaves in early summer from third year

FIG You can train fig plants as fans in much the same way as peaches (see page 58). They are, however, even more space-demanding, and in the smaller greenhouse are better grown as bushes in large pots or tubs. Cut the young fig tree back to 450 mm (18 in) in autumn. A year later, treat all the young stems the same way. From then on, pinch back all shoots to three leaves in early summer. Subsequent growth will bear the fruits: no pollination is required. In autumn cut back the fruited stems to 50 mm (2 in) and the non-fruited ones to half their length.

The bushes should be re-potted every year in autumn using John Innes Potting No 3. After the early summer pinching, apply a liquid feed every week until the fruit is picked. In the normal way, the plants should be kept cool. On the other hand, you can gently **force** the fig crop if you maintain a minimum temperature of 13°C (55°F) from January. If you remove the fruited stems immediately after harvesting, you will get two (and possibly three) crops each year.

MELON

The melon can be a rewarding summer fruit crop. It is grown in much the same way as the cucumber, but it needs full sun. Manure is not essential and the growing mounds can be made of a good potting mixture, such as John Innes No 2 or 3; alternatively, you can use 250-300 mm (10-12 in) pots. Support the plants in the same way as for cucumbers.

Sow the seeds edgeways-on (below, left) in small pots at 24°C (75°F) in late spring. When the young plants have two or three leaves they can be set in the mounds (below, right). As the main stem grows, **train** it vertically. Tie in the lateral stems horizontally, pinching back each one at the fifth leaf. The sublateral shoots produce most of the fruits. There are separate male and female flowers and pollination must be done by hand. If the petals of the male flower are removed, the club-like pollen mass can be used as a brush to dust the stigma of the female flower. To get an even development of fruits, you must pollinate at least six well-placed female flowers within a few days of each other. (It might be thought that pollinating over a longer period would usefully extend the time of ripening. In practice, however, one is liable to finish up with a few, large fruits and a number of very small, late-maturing ones that are hardly worth having.)

Each plant can produce four good-sized fruits or six smaller ones; any others should be removed while they are still small. As soon as the fruits start to swell, begin liquid feeding once a week. When the fruits are the size of small oranges, support each in a hammock of netting firmly attached to the supporting wires. As soon as the fruits cease swelling, reduce the watering so that the soil is kept barely moist. At this stage the leaves may yellow or wither. The fruits are ready to gather when they start to give off the characteristic melon fragrance.

Pinching out leading shoot
(right) and laterals (below)

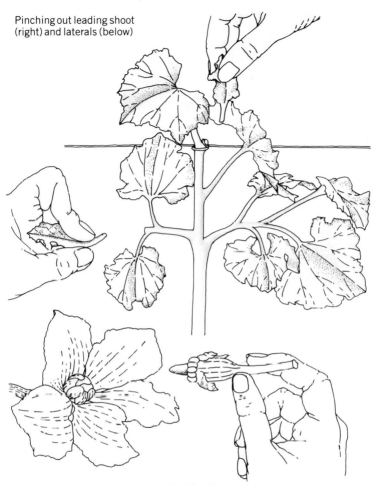

Above: pollinate female flower (left) with pollen mass of the male flower

Right: net hammock
for melon

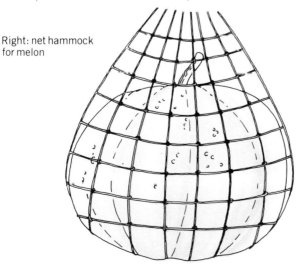

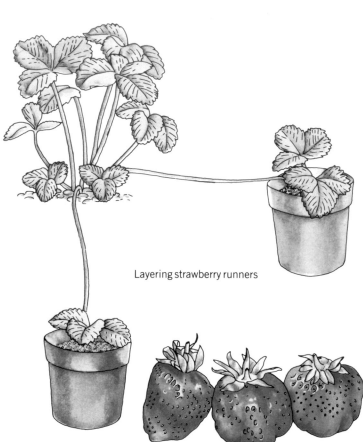

Layering strawberry runners

STRAWBERRY
Although it is hardy, the strawberry plant responds well to early warmth and can be fruited in the greenhouse well ahead of its normal season. Young, vigorous plants are obtained by layering runners in 100 mm (4 in) pots of good potting compost as early in the season as possible. When the plants are well rooted, pot them on into 150 mm (6 in) pots of John Innes Potting No 2, and make sure to grow them in a sheltered place. Strawberry plants must never lack water, and when they are well grown they should be fed at 10-day intervals until September. During October they are kept on the dry side for about three weeks. In December remove all dead and dying leaves and bring the plants into a cold greenhouse.

If you want a really early crop you must provide the plants with artificial heat – a minimum of 7°C (45°F) is essential – from early January onwards. Liquid feeding at weekly intervals should start as soon as the flowers open, and the flowers must be hand-pollinated with a soft brush.

FORCING CROPS Chicory, seakale, asparagus, and rhubarb can be conveniently forced under the benching of a cool or warm greenhouse. You can raise a supply of roots for these in the garden. Exclude light from the growing area with heavy-duty black plastic sheeting; alternatively, you can use a light-proof box.

Chicory and seakale roots are lifted in batches from late autumn onwards. Cut the leaves back to 12 mm (½ in) and trim the roots to 250 mm (10 in). Pack the roots 50 mm (2 in) apart in pots or boxes of moist peat or sandy soil.

Asparagus is lifted in January or February; the roots are only lightly trimmed, and then are packed around with soil under the bench. Rhubarb is lifted in late autumn and left lying outside the greenhouse until it has experienced several frosts. It is then dealt with as for asparagus.

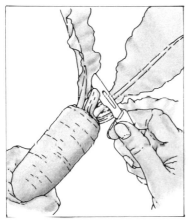

Dig up chicory roots when leaves die from mid-October.

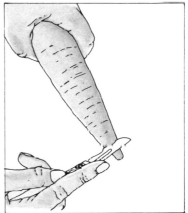

Trim root ends and cut leaves to 12 mm (½ in) above crown.

Put roots in deep box or pot of moist peat or sandy soil.

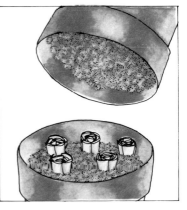

Exclude light for 3-4 weeks; store at 10-13°C (50-56°F)

CHRYSANTHEMUMS

Essentially, these are part-time greenhouse plants: they need bench space for propagation in spring and for flowering in autumn and early winter. Although they are perennials, chrysanthemums are best grown annually from cuttings.

Previous season's plants that were overwintered in a frost-free frame or greenhouse are given a minimum temperature of 7°C (45°F) in January. When the new shoots are 50-62 mm (2-2½ in) long, they are removed at ground level. **Pinch off** the lower leaves and sever the base cleanly with a razor blade or sharp knife.

Loosely fill pots or boxes and gently push in the cuttings at 50 mm (2 in) intervals. After giving them a thorough watering, place them in a propagator. As soon as they have rooted and resumed growth, set them singly into 90 mm (3½ in) pots of

In early spring select a new chrysanthemum shoot for propagation.

Pinch off the lower leaves of the cutting; take care not to strip any skin from the stem.

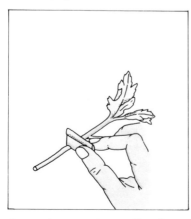

Sever the stem immediately below one of the leaf joints with a razor blade.

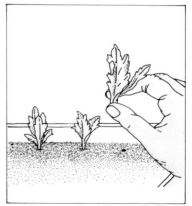

Insert cuttings 50 mm (2 in) apart in cutting compost and place them in a propagator.

John Innes Potting No 2.

When they are about 200 mm (8 in) tall, pinch them out to promote branching. As soon as they are well developed, pot the plants on into 150 mm (6 in) containers and provide each with a short cane support.

The plants are hardened off and stood outside in May. Choose a sheltered site and erect a **wire support system.** About midsummer day, the plants should be stopped again and potted on into their final 250 mm (10 in) pots containing John Innes Potting No 3.

The short canes must be supplemented with 1.2 m (4 ft) ones, which should be secured to the wires to prevent wind damage. Approximately six weeks after the final potting, begin fortnightly feeding with an approved chrysanthemum fertiliser. At all times make sure that the plants do not lack water.

Above: pinch out above first full leaves to aid branching

Right: in midsummer remove all buds except topmost from side shoots at the leaf axils

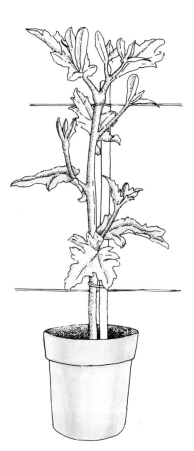

Disbudding: for large single flowers, pinch out all buds below the main central one

Once growth is under way after the **second pinching**, examine each plant carefully and remove all but the strongest six to nine stems. Supporting ties must go out to each stem, or separate canes can be provided. If large, solitary flowers are required – and all the most popular cultivars are of this type – **disbudding** must be carried out. When the bud clusters appear, carefully pinch out all buds except the large central one. If you want sprays of smaller flowers, however, allow all the buds to mature. As soon as there is fear of frost, bring the plants into the greenhouse. It is wise to spray them beforehand against pests such as aphids. Ventilate the greenhouse freely to prevent day temperatures from rising above 18-21°C (65-70°F). Night temperatures should not be above 7°C (45°F). After flowering the plants are cut back and kept just moist until January.

FUCHSIA The many varieties of fuchsia, with their attractive pendulous flowers, make splendid pot plants for the beginner and expert alike. The fuchsia is a shrub and can be kept for several years in the same-sized container if it is regularly re-potted and hard-pruned in late winter. Alternatively, it can be grown annually or biennially from cuttings; these are stem tips or small side shoots about 50-75 mm (2-3 in) long which can be taken from late spring to late summer. Plants will grow and flower in winter if a 10-13°C (50-55°F) minimum temperature is maintained in the greenhouse. Otherwise, they can be kept almost dry and overwintered in a frost-free house.

The young plants will need to be pinched several times to promote bushy specimens. Pyramids are grown as follows: the young plants are pinched out at 150 mm (6 in) and the strongest of the resulting shoots is tied vertically to a 1.2 m (4 ft) cane. When this leading stem is 150 mm (6 in) long it is pinched again and another strong shoot is tied erect. This is continued until the desired height is reached. All fuchsias need regular watering and feeding. Lax-growing sorts make good hanging-basket specimens.

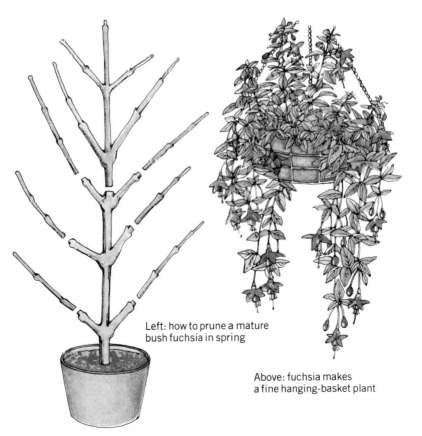

Left: how to prune a mature bush fuchsia in spring

Above: fuchsia makes a fine hanging-basket plant

CARNATIONS

Perpetual-flowering carnations will bloom in the depth of winter if a minimum night temperature of 10°C (50°F) can be maintained. The plants are almost hardy, however, and will survive in just frost-free conditions. Young plants are best obtained in spring and placed in 125 mm (5 in) pots of a reliable potting compost. A 900 mm (3 ft) cane should be inserted for support. Wire carnation rings are obtainable and save tying. If flowers are required as soon as possible the plants are allowed to develop naturally. When grown in this way, perpetual carnation plants will usually grow long, with very little natural branching except high up on the stem. Unlike the effect with most other plants, pinching out the soft stem tips of carnations does not encourage a sufficient number of new branches and snapping must be carried out. Stems are allowed to grow about 100 mm (4 in) beyond the point at which branching is required and are then snapped off sideways (below, left). A cluster of evenly sized lateral stems will then develop just below that point. If a main flush of bloom is

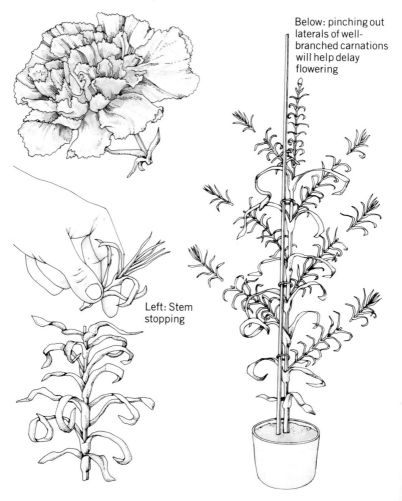

Below: pinching out laterals of well-branched carnations will help delay flowering

Left: Stem stopping

required in late summer, the top is **stopped** (snapped off) when the plants are about 250 mm (10 in) tall. If the resultant shoots are again stopped, the main display will be in winter. Alternatively, the floral display can be spread over a longer period by stopping some shoots and leaving others.

When the plants have filled the 125 mm (5 in) pots with roots, usually when they are about 450 mm (18 in) tall, they must be moved into 175 or 200 mm (7 or 8 in) pots. A supplementary 1.5 m (5 ft) cane can be provided at this time. When the flower buds show, begin liquid feeding at 10- to 14-day intervals. The flower buds are borne in clusters and if large flowers are required the small side buds must be removed by snapping them out sideways.

Cuttings can be taken at any time of the year, but late winter or late summer are the best times. Cuttings are easily obtained by snapping or cutting-off non-flowering shoot tips, removing the lower leaves, and inserting the tips in pots of coarse sand in a propagating frame with bottom heat at 18-21°C (65-70°F).

Select a shoot for a cutting; cut it close to the stem.

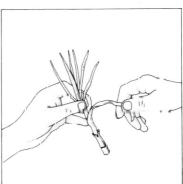

Strip off lower leaves by pulling them downwards.

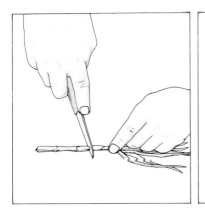

Trim cutting just below joint of highest stripped leaf.

Insert cuttings around edge of pot filled with sand.

PELARGONIUMS

The botanical name *Pelargonium* covers three distinct groups of plants. Best known of these is the geranium, with round, often bronze-zoned leaves and large heads of flowers (above, left). Less familiar is the regal or show pelargonium (above, right) with its sharp-toothed, somewhat cupped leaves and smaller clusters of relatively large flowers that are often bicoloured. Popular for hanging baskets is the trailing ivy-leaved group, with deeply lobed leaves and heads of narrow-petalled blooms. Regals need a minimum temperature of 7-10°C (45-50°F); the others will survive at 5°C (40°F) if kept on the dry side. If winter blooms of geranium are required, a temperature of 10°C (50°F) must be provided. All three types respond to good winter light and will grow in any proprietary compost. Good plants can be flowered in 150-200 mm (6-8 in) pots. Propagation is by 75-100 mm (3-4 in) cuttings taken in late summer or spring, the latter if there is not much heat in winter. Young plants need pinching to promote bushiness, and should be fed every week in summer.

Preparing a geranium stem tip as a cutting: remove lower leaves and small stipules at bases of leaf-stalks.

BEGONIA

The begonias can be divided into two main groups, tuberous (above, left) and fibrous-rooted (above, right). The latter is represented by the large double (rose) flowered cultivars and the smaller, Pendula types so useful for hanging baskets. In the fibrous groups are many fine plants including the ornamental-leaved Rex hybrids and the winter flowering Lorraine selections. Lorraine has been crossed with the tuberous kinds to create large-flowered winter bloomers known as the Hiemalis or Elatior group.

All the winter flowerers need a winter minimum of 7-10°C (45-50°F) and thrive in 125-150 mm (5-6 in) pots of peat compost. They must be cut back in late winter and kept on the dry side for 4-6 weeks. Normal watering is then resumed and the temperature maintained at around 18°C (65°F). Resultant shoots are taken as cuttings. All other begonias can be propagated by stem or leaf cuttings in late spring or summer. Tuberous types can be grown from year to year. The corms are started in trays of moist peat at 18°C (65°F) in spring. As the leaves start to expand they are potted singly into 150-200 mm (6-8 in) containers, the Pendulas three together in 250 mm (10 in) hanging baskets. When flowers buds show, feeding at 7-10 day intervals should start. Restrict the large double-flowered cultivars to one or two stems, which must be securely staked as the plants can become top heavy. When the foliage yellows in autumn they are dried off and stored at not less than 7°C (45°F).

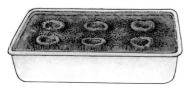

Start tuberous begonia corms in trays of moist peat.

When leaves begin to expand, pot young begonias singly.

OTHER POT PLANTS A number of half-hardy or
tender annuals and short-lived perennials are among the
indispensable groups that provide the most popular flowering
pot plants – notably calceolaria, cyclamen, cineraria *(Senecio)*,
Primula malacoides (fairy primrose), *P. obconica*, and
Schizanthus (poor-man's orchid). All of these require cool
greenhouse conditions and will thrive in John Innes or any
other reliable compost. All are grown annually from seeds,
although cyclamen can subsequently be propagated by corms.
Calceolaria is sown about midsummer in a shady cold frame.
The seedlings are pricked off as soon as they are large enough
to handle, and later they are set singly in 90 mm (3½ in) pots.
When they are well grown they must be potted-on into 125 or
150 mm (5 or 6 in) pots. Ventilate the greenhouse freely on
sunny days. As soon as the nights begin to cool in autumn,
artificial heat must be provided. If you want really big plants
they can be put in larger pots in late winter. Either way, the
plants must be fed at 7-10 day intervals from early spring.

Schizanthus

Cineraria

Primula malacoides

This pattern of cultivation can be followed for the other plants mentioned above, with the following modifications. Sow cyclamen seeds in early autumn for big plants, in spring for smaller ones. An all-peat compost is best. Autumn-sown plants can be flowered in 175 mm (7 in) pots, spring sown ones in 90 or 130 mm pots (3½ or 5 in) pots. They are dried off in late spring and repotted in late summer. Make sure that the top half of each corn is just above the surface of the compost, and water sparingly until the young leaves are well developed. Thereafter, avoid watering into the centre of the plant. Primulas are sown and treated as for calceolarias; larger, earlier-flowering plants will result if they are sown in spring. Cineraria is sown in spring for winter flowering, in summer for the following late spring/early summer. The plants can be kept in an open frame all summer if screened from the hottest sun. *Schizanthus* is sown in late summer, and for big specimens three plants are set in 175-200 mm (7-8 in) pots. Twiggy supports and good winter light are needed for shapely, floriferous plants.

Cyclamen

Primula obconica

BULBS

Bulbous-rooted plants are ideal for rapidly providing colourful pot plants. They are particularly valuable for creating winter interest in the barely heated or unheated greenhouse which is largely devoted to summer crops. **Hardy bulbs** are needed for this purpose, and among the most suitable are crocus, daffodil, narcissus, tulip and hyacinth (below, left). In early autumn they are set fairly close together in pots or pans of a proprietary compost and plunged in sand, peat or ashes in a shady cold frame or under a north wall. This encourages a good root system to form. In early December they are brought into the greenhouse. Artificial heat is needed only to keep out severe frost. On sunny days the greenhouse must be freely ventilated. If feeding is given when the flower buds show and at 14-day intervals until they fade, the bulbs can be used from year to year. When the flowers finish the pots should be placed in a cold frame and kept moist until the foliage dies down.

Bulb growing: crocks stop compost leaking out of holes.

Plant bulbs so that one third shows above compost.

Plunge pots in peat in well ventilated frame.

Several **tender bulbs** make a bright display in the cool greenhouse. They are all potted as described above but kept in the cool greenhouse and watered sparingly until growth gets underway. From then on they are watered and fed as required and dried off when the foliage yellows. Especially recommended, the following are potted in late summer to early autumn: *Lachenalia* (Cape cowslip), freesia, and nerine, the first two needing annual re-potting; canna, gloriosa, *Polianthes* (tuberose), smithiantha, and tigridia, all potted and re-potted annually in spring; *Vallota* (Scarborough lily), potted in summer, and *Hippeastrum* (amaryllis), potted in summer or autumn, both re-potted only every third year.

An *en-masse* display of these summer bulbs can create a delightful spectacle. They can also be used to add variety to a mixed collection; a particularly effective way to use them is as specimens among ferns and other foliage plants.

Tender bulbs for display in a cool greenhouse: left, freesia makes a fragrant and colourful display in the early spring; right, Cape cowslip (*Lachenalia*) develops elegant tubular bell flowers, February to May

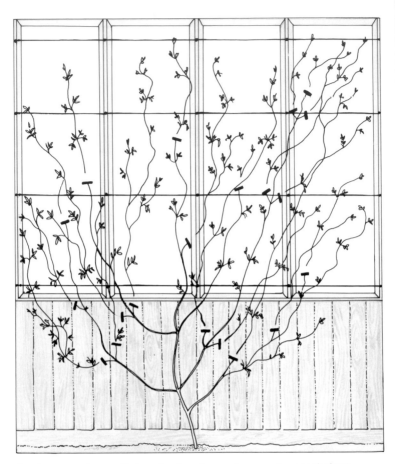

Pruning a greenhouse climber, showing where cuts are made on each shoot

ORNAMENTAL CLIMBERS
Flowering climbing plants trained into the roof space can provide a particularly attractive and satisfying greenhouse feature. Alternatively they can be grown flat on the wall of a lean-to, or trained up netting or sticks. Vine eyes and galvanised wires make the best support system (see page 45). Climbers should ideally be permanently planted in the greenhouse border, but they can also be grown in tubs or large pots; for the latter any reliable potting compost can be used. **Top dressing** (see page 42) of both containers and borders must be done every year in early spring, and the plants must be fed fortnightly in summer.

If possible, plant in the spring. If the young plant has only a few stems it should be cut back by half to promote branching. The resulting new stems should be tied to the supports in a narrow fan formation; stem tips can be pinched-out to stimulate further branching. In this way a framework of permanent stems will become established. Side shoots (laterals) from these stems will produce a canopy of foliage and

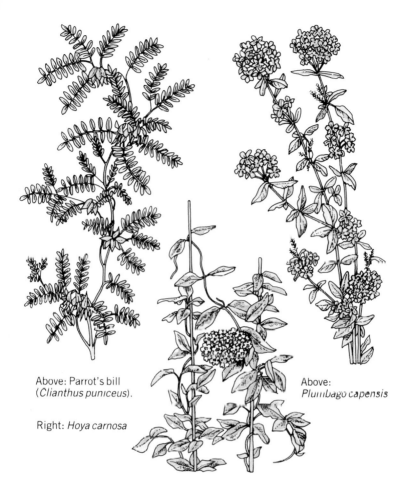

Above: Parrot's bill
(*Clianthus puniceus*).

Right: *Hoya carnosa*

Above:
Plumbago capensis

flowers. Annual **pruning** consists of removing dead flowers
when necessary and drastically thinning and cutting back the
laterals in late winter.

The following species are well worth trying. Frost-free
greenhouse: *Clianthus puniceus* (parrot's bill) is a slender
shrub grown as a climber with dissected (pinnate) leaves and
large pendant beak-shaped red or white flowers in spring;
Jasminum polyanthum resembles the common hardy jasmine
but has pinkish buds and more fragrant flowers in spring (in a
cool greenhouse it will bloom in winter). Cool greenhouse:
Hoya carnosa (wax flower) has fleshy-leathery, glossy leaves
and hanging clusters of waxy, fragrant, white and pink stars all
summer; *Plumbago capensis* is best known for its long
succession of flowers which resemble sky-blue primroses;
Steptosolen jamesonii (marmalade bush) is a climber which in
late spring becomes smothered with delightful tubular,
bright orange flowers; *Lapageria rosea* (Chilean bellflower)
has very attractive, waxy, rose-crimson bell flowers.

SUCCULENTS

SUCCULENTS The unique shapes and often beautiful flowers of cacti and other succulent plants have a wide appeal. As greenhouse plants they are an ideal interest for those often away from home as they will stand wide fluctuations of temperature and moisture. They will not, however, thrive on neglect, and to get vigorous growth and regular flowering the following routine should be observed. A sunny, frost-free greenhouse is required, freely ventilated once the temperature exceeds 21°C (70°F). Keep the plants dry from late October to April, then water them regularly but allow the compost to almost dry out between applications. From late spring to late summer, liquid feed should be given at 14-day intervals to all well-established specimens.

Propagation by **cuttings** is carried out in summer. Mature stem-tips or pads – the pear-shaped constricted stems of *Opuntia* (prickly pear) – are severed and allowed to dry in the sun for a few days, then they are inserted in pots of coarse sand and kept just moist. When they have rooted, place them singly in pots of any proprietary potting compost, preferably mixed with one third part coarse sand or fine grit. As the plants grow, pot them on or re-pot them in spring. Prickly cacti and their cuttings can be handled more easily if you make a 'collar' from a rolled-up newspaper. In addition to the familiar desert cacti there are those that are epiphytic, climbing or perching on mossy tree branches. In the greenhouse they need a more peaty compost and must be shaded in summer. Some of the best known examples, such as *Epiphyllum*, Christmas, and Easter cacti, make excellent hanging-basket specimens. All need a minimum winter temperature of 7-10°C (45-50°F).

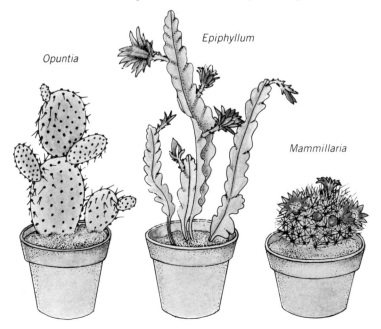

Opuntia

Epiphyllum

Mammillaria

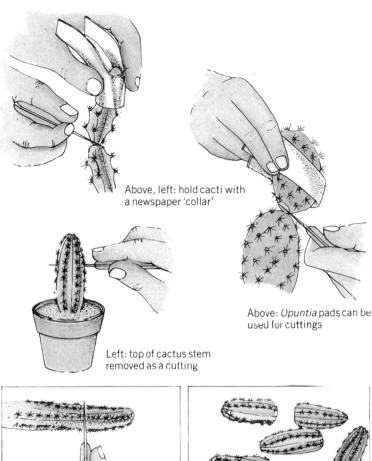

Above, left: hold cacti with a newspaper 'collar'

Above: *Opuntia* pads can be used for cuttings

Left: top of cactus stem removed as a cutting

Preparing cuttings: slice off stem pieces cleanly.

Allow cuttings to dry in the sun for a few days.

After drying, insert them in barely moist, coarse sand.

When they have made roots put into compost/sand mix.

ORCHIDS

ORCHIDS Although orchid culture is surrounded by a certain amount of mystique, there are many different kinds with which the beginner can succeed. Great heat is not necessary and some of the best orchids thrive with a winter minimum of 7°C (45°F). Most of the popular greenhouse orchids are epiphytes growing on mossy tree branches. Many of them have swollen, bulb-like stems called pseudo-bulbs which act as food and water reserves. They require a well-aerated and drained **compost.** Traditionally the main ingredient of this has been chopped fern roots (osmunda fibre). This is now very expensive and has been largely superseded by chips of fir-tree and other barks and by plastic chips (nodules). A recommended mix is two parts bark chips and one part (by bulk) sphagnum moss, both available from garden centres.

Special **perforated pans** or **baskets** should be used, or the plants can be secured to slabs of tree-fern stem. When potting,

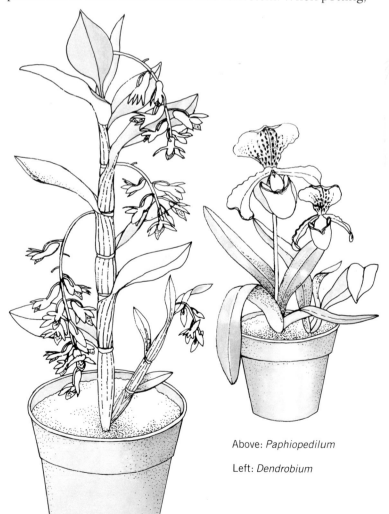

Above: *Paphiopedilum*

Left: *Dendrobium*

work in some of the compost among the thick, rubbery roots, then partially coil and insert these into the container. Fill in more compost around the roots and lightly firm it. Watering is best achieved by dunking the containers in water for several seconds. The compost should just about have dried out before each watering. The plants need very little water in winter.

Re-potting should take place every three or four years in early autumn or spring. Well-established plants benefit from a half-strength liquid feed at 2- to 3-week intervals while new growth forms. **Division** is the easiest means of propagation and is carried out just as new growth starts in spring. The clumps of bulbs need to be severed carefully with a sharp knife.

Among the most popular genera for the cool greenhouse are: *Cymbidium, Dendrobium, Laelia,* and *Paphiopedilum (Cypripedium). Cattleya* species need a night minimum temperature of 10-13°C (50-55°F).

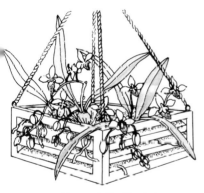

Above: slatted basket

Below: perforated pot

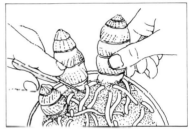

Orchid division. detach a back-bulb with its roots.

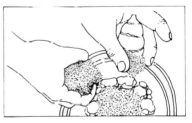

Put back-bulb in gravel-lined pot half full of compost.

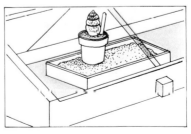

Place pot on bed of moist sand in propagator.

FRAMES & CLOCHES

FRAMES These can play a variety of roles in the garden. In conjunction with a greenhouse they can act as an overflow and **hardening-off** centre for plants eventually to be grown outside. By themselves they can be used for all of the shorter plants normally cultivated in a greenhouse. They can also be used for producing **early vegetables** such as lettuce, carrots, and turnips, and for summer crops of cucumbers and melons. A close watch must be kept on ventilation, as the comparatively small volume of air can rapidly overheat in direct sunlight. Frames are available in a wide variety of styles and sizes. Of those shown here, the traditional wooden-box type is generally the cheapest and remains as useful as any. Some versions have asbestos sides. The modern glass-sided design with a span roof can be recommended for light-demanding winter crops such as lettuce. Another use for frames, whether heated or unheated, is for **propagation.** With a 100-150 mm (4-6 in) layer of coarse sand in the bottom and with adequate shade from the sun in summer, you can root cuttings of both hardy and half-hardy plants. In addition, many different kinds of seeds can be germinated.

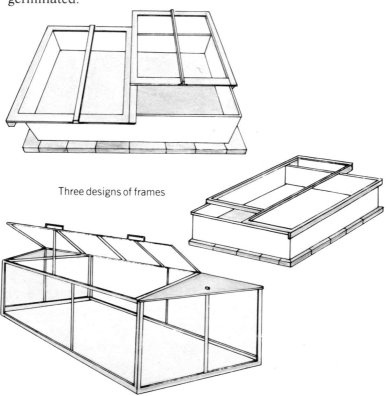

Three designs of frames

GARDEN FRAME CROPS

PLANTS GROWN TO MATURITY

NAME	SOWN	MINIMUM TEMP.	REMARKS
Radish	February	7°C (45°F)	All these
Carrot	February	7-10°C (45-50°F)	plants are
Turnip	February	7-10°C (45-50F)	grown to
Spinach	February	7-10°C (45-50°F)	maturity
Beetroot	February	7-10°C (45-50°F)	where they
French beans	February	10-15°C (50-55°F)	are sown
Tomato	March	16-18°C (60-65°F)	
Cucumber	April	21-26°C (70-80°F)	
Primula obconica	April-May	7-10°C (45-50°F)	
Calceolaria	June	7-10°C (45-50°F)	
Cineraria *(Senecio)*	June	10-13°C (50-55°F)	
Primula malacoides	June	7-10°C (45-50°F)	
Cyclamen	August	10-13°C (50-55°F)	
Lettuce	September	10°C (50°F)	

NAME	POTTED	BROUGHT IN	MINIMUM TEMP.
Hardy bulbs	Sept-Oct	Nov-Dec	5°C (40°F)
Hardy perennials (violet, astilbe, dicentra, etc)	October	January	5-7°C (40-45°F)
Rhubarb		December	13-15°C (55-60°F)
Seakale		November	10-13°C (50-55°F)
Chicory		November	10-13°C (50-55°F)
Asparagus		February	10-13°C (50-55°F)

PLANTS RAISED FOR THE OPEN GARDEN

NAME	SOWN	CUTTINGS	MINIMUM TEMP.
Hardy annuals	Oct; Feb		13°C (55°F)
Cabbage	February		10°C (50°F)
Cauliflower	Sept; Feb		10°C (50°F)
Half-hardy annuals (lobelia, petunia, tagetes, etc)	February March		13-16°C (55-60°F) 18°C (65°F)
Tender perennials (heliotrope, dahlia, etc)	Feb-Mar February	September Feb-Mar	18°C (65°F) 18°C (65°F)
Hardy perennials (delphinium, lupin, etc)	March March	March March	5-7°C (40-45°F) 5-7°C (40-45°F)
Hardy shrubs		July-Sept	16-21°C (65-70°F)

CLOCHES

Although cloches can be used for some of the same purposes as frames, their primary use is for extending the growing season of food crops in the open garden. With the aid of such protective covering, vegetable seeds can be sown earlier and the resulting plants will grow more rapidly. Cloches are particularly valuable for raising young plants of half-hardy vegetables, notably sweet-corn, marrow, and ridge cucumber. In colder areas or in cold, wet summers you could succeed even in an open site by growing permanently under cloches crops such as cucumber, tomato, and melon. Even if the summer is warm enough for these plants to grow without cover, cloches can ensure a longer season of ripening if they are put in position with the coming of the cool nights of early autumn. Flowers, too, can benefit from cloche protection. Hardy

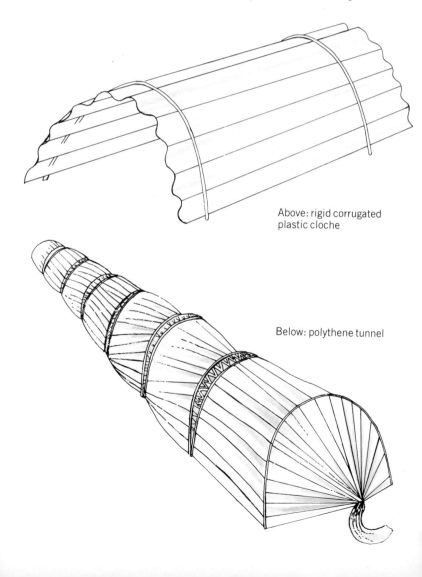

Above: rigid corrugated plastic cloche

Below: polythene tunnel

annuals needed for cut flowers can be sown under them in early autumn and will flower earlier the following year. Anemone corms planted in summer will continue flowering well into winter, as will the normally autumn-blooming Kaffir lily *(Schizostylis)* if it is protected against the worst weather.

Many different **designs** of cloches are available in both glass and plastic sheeting. Shown here is a simple span type useful for early vegetable sowing, and a larger barn type suitable for growing to maturity plants such as tomato and egg plant (aubergine). The polythene-sheeting cloche with rigid framework and the tunnel cloche have the same uses. The latter consists of a long strip of polythene sheeting over a supporting framework of inverted-U-shaped wires or canes; it is particularly useful for forcing strawberries.

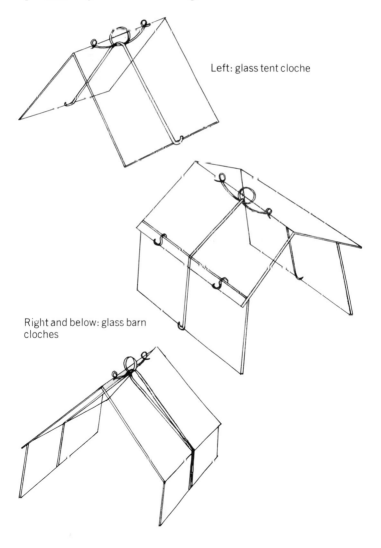

Left: glass tent cloche

Right and below: glass barn cloches

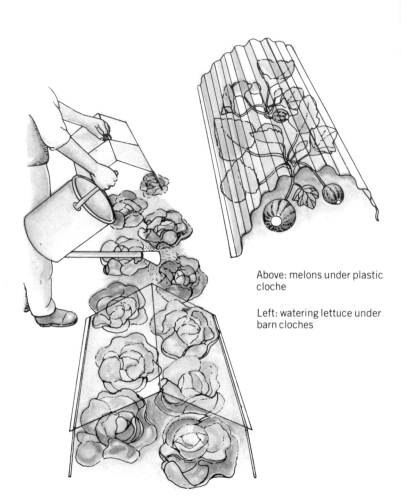

Above: melons under plastic cloche

Left: watering lettuce under barn cloches

CROPS UNDER CLOCHES
The basic cultural preparations for growing plants under cloches are the same as those for unprotected crops. Remove all perennial weeds, then dig, manure, firm, and rake the soil to a fine seed-sowing tilth. Ideally, you should put the cloches in position at least two weeks before sowing or planting so that they can warm up the soil. During the autumn-to-spring period the cloches should be butted end to end. In summer, all cloches that do not have an opening device should be placed with a 25 mm (1 in) gap between them to prevent the plants overheating. You can provide extra protection and head-room by setting the cloches over a shallow, flat-bottomed trench in which sowing and planting has been carried out. Tunnel cloches are ventilated by pushing up the sheeting on the side away from the direction of the wind. Watering can be an awkward operation. Unless your cloches are designed for watering in situ, the easiest method is to remove the end-of-row cloche and move the remainder

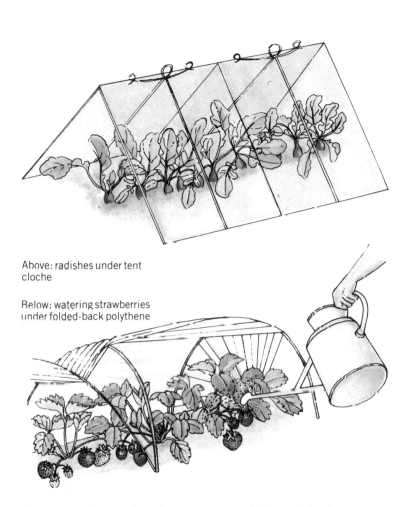

Above: radishes under tent
cloche

Below: watering strawberries
under folded-back polythene

along one place as the plants are soaked. Tunnel cloches are
watered from the side.

Cloches should never be idle in the autumn-to-spring period.
Lettuces sown in the open in August can be covered in
September for cutting in late autumn. Salad onions sown in
August and covered in late September will mature well ahead
of time in the following spring. More lettuces can be sown in
late September to over-winter under cover and mature in
spring. In cold areas, peas and broad beans can be sown and
covered about mid-October. A first sowing of radish and turnip
can be made in February and continued at 2- to 3-week
intervals. Tomato needs heat to germinate properly and should
be sown in March. Young plants can be hardened off and put
under cloches in May. Egg plant and sweet peppers can be
treated in the same way. Marrow (courgette-type) can be
similarly dealt with if sowing in April, or can be sown under
cloches in May.

PESTS & DISEASES

DAMAGE CAUSED	NAME AND APPEARANCE	CONTROL
Leaves and young shoots curled or deformed.	Green and blackfly (aphids), crowded tiny soft-bodied greenish to black insects	Derris, malathion
Leaves with a yellowish mottling and sometimes a fine webbing.	Glasshouse red-spider mite, microscopic spider-like red-spotted creatures	Formothion, malathion, plus extra humidity
Leaves with pale sinuous tracks or lines, especially on chrysanthemum.	Chrysanthemum leaf-mining fly, the tiny grub of which feeds between the upper and lower leaf skins.	HCH (BHC), nicotine
Leaves of amaryllis *(Hippeastrum)* with red or rusty streaks and distortion	Bulb-scale mite, a microscopic colourless creature living within the bulb.	Plants should be discarded and burnt.
Leaves with white flies and/or tiny yellowish scales.	Glasshouse whitefly, a pure white tiny moth-like fly, the scale-like grub feeding on sap. See also next entry.	HCH (BHC), or a natural parasite *(Encarsia)*.
Leaves with blackish sticky film.	Sooty mould, a fungus which grows on the sticky honey dew exuded by whitefly grubs and scale insects.	Gently swab with warm water. Kill pests.
Leaves of stems with brownish or whitish scales.	Scale insects, oval to mussel-shaped flat insects which suck sap. See also previous entry.	Equal parts nicotine and petroleum oil.
Leaves of tomato blotched yellow above and brownish or purplish beneath	Leaf-mould disease, aggravated by very warm, humid conditions.	Liquid copper, zineb. Grow only resistant cultivated varieties.

DAMAGE CAUSED	NAME AND APPEARANCE	CONTROL
Leaves and young shoots wilting.	1. Vine weevil, the fat white grub stage eating roots. 2. Root mealy bug, like stem mealy bug but feeds on root. 3. Root-rot disease; killing and browning caused by over-watering.	1. Water with HCH (BHC). 2. Water with formothion or nicotine. 3. Discard if all roots are brown.
Leaves and stems browning, then with a grey or whitish fluffy mould.	Grey-mould disease *(Botrytis)*, usually attacking damaged tissue, especially under humid cool conditions.	Dust with captan and maintain dryer atmosphere.
Stems with whitish or pinkish woolly masses.	Mealy bugs, soft oval insects with a waxy woolly covering, often in colonies, which suck sap and weaken the plant.	Spray with diazinon; swab woody stems with a 50-50 mixture of nicotine and methylated spirits.
Seedlings collapsing at soil level.	Damping-off disease which kills the stem base and is aggravated by overcrowding and wet conditions.	Water with captan or zineb. Sow seeds thinly.
Flower buds withering, yellowing, or falling prematurely.	Various causes: dryness at the root; sudden sharp changes in temperature; over-warm conditions.	Regulate temperatures and make sure plants never lack water.
Tomato fruits with blossom end brownish-black.	Blossom-end rot, caused by lack of adequate lime and dryness at the root.	Make sure plants never dry out and apply lime at planting time.
Tomato fruits with hard unripe areas.	Blotchy ripening, caused by over-high temperatures and lack of potash.	Regulate temperatures and use a special tomato fertiliser.

PESTS AND DISEASES

Whether they are grown by a beginner or by an expert, from time to time plants are attacked by pests and diseases or suffer from cultural defects. All too often the worst pests and diseases enter the greenhouse on plants acquired from friends or from inefficient nurseries, so always make a point of examining thoroughly all new plants before taking them into the greenhouse. The greatest nuisances are red-spider mites, whitefly, mealy bug, and greenfly (see below). Although small numbers of them can sometimes be dealt with by squashing or by swilling around in warm soapy water, more usually a chemical cure is required. Always read the instructions on the insecticide or fungicide container carefully and carry them out to the letter: a pesticide used at a greater concentration than recommended could damage the plant; too weak a mixture may be a waste of time. If you use a spray, take care to apply the solution only to the affected plants. Remember when buying that some of the newer preparations

Greenhouse pests. Above: red spider mite sucks leaf sap.

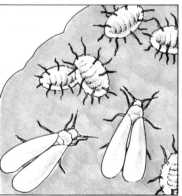

Whitefly larva sucks sap and excretes 'honeydew'.

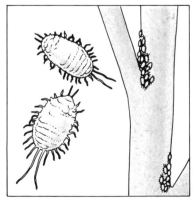

Mealy bug attacks vines, succulents, and other plants.

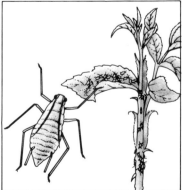

Greenfly (here) and blackfly, common sap-sucking aphids.

have not been tested on a wide range of greenhouse plants. Fungicides and insecticides are available in various forms: as liquids applied to the soil (systemic), as liquids sprayed onto foliage, as dusting powders, and as fumigant smokes applied via pyrotechnic canisters or 'bombs'. For fumigants, the greenhouse must be closed tightly; evening is the best time to use them. For a few pests, notably red-spider mite and whitefly, it is now possible to obtain natural predatory insects for biological control; but these are not easy to employ in the small greenhouse as they quickly die out and so may need to be introduced several times during the season.

Many substances now used to kill pest and disease organisms are marketed under more than one brand name. In the chart on pages 92-3, the chemical names of the active ingredients are used. Your local horticultural shop or garden centre will be able to identify for you the various brands that are based on these ingredients.

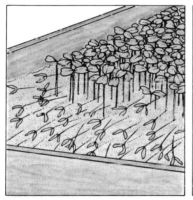

Damping-off, a common disease of seedlings in trays.

Tomato leaf mould forms yellow patch on upper side.

Above: always spray under surfaces of leaves when using insecticides. Right: fumigants are ideal for the greenhouse.

INDEX